writing & selling your
memoir

WRITER'S DIGEST
BOOK

WritersDigest
Cincinnati, O

writing & selling your
memoir

PAULA BALZER

To receive a free weekly e-mail newsletter delivering tips and updates about writing and about Writer's Digest products, register directly at http://newsletters.fw publications.com.

15 14 13 12 11   5 4 3 2 1

Distributed in Canada by Fraser Direct
100 Armstrong Avenue
Georgetown, Ontario, Canada L7G 5S4
Tel: (905) 877-4411

Distributed in the U.K. and Europe by F&W Media International, LTD
Brunel House, Forde Close, Newton Abbot, Devon, TQ12 4PU, UK
Tel: (+44) 1626-323200, Fax: (+44) 1626-323319
E-mail: enquiries@fwmedia.com

Distributed in Australia by Capricorn Link
P.O. Box 704, Windsor, NSW 2756 Australia
Tel: (02) 4577-3555

Edited by Scott Francis
Designed by Claudean Wheeler
Photographs by Jason Bash
Production coordinated by Debbie Thomas

Dedication

TO PETER: Because my best stories start with you.

AND JUNE: Who added new chapters, better chapters—who would have thought?

table of contents

INTRODUCTION:
Why Write Your Memoir?

can still remember the day that I first fell in love with a memoir. It was on a day much like today in fact—a cold day, relentless with rain. I had been living in New York City for about a year, had my first post-college job, and was living in a tiny studio apartment that I adored despite its many pitfalls. While I was lucky to be gainfully employed (somewhat gainfully anyway) and to have found a semi-decent place to live, I still hadn't been here long enough to fully integrate myself into my new hometown. New York was exciting yes, but tough going at times. It was lonely, and I often felt like I was the only person in an entire city of six million who didn't have a few friends she could call up to have brunch or make plans to see a movie. So, books were my solace, and I tore through them like crazy that first year. Stocking up on a few novels on Sunday afternoons became a ritual, and it was during a visit to Brooklyn's BookCourt that I happened upon Mary Cantwell's *Manhattan, When I Was Young*. While I can't honestly say it was the first memoir I had read, I know it's the first one that made a lasting impression. I immediately connected with Cantwell's story of moving to New York City to work in publishing, even though her affair with the city started a good forty years before mine did. I felt an instant kinship with her narrative that was unlike anything I had felt when reading fiction. Like all book lovers, I have my favorite characters, and have found myself closely relating to Beverly Cleary's charming, though undeniably awkward, Ramona Quimby since the age of eight. On a good day, I might feel a bit like Harper Lee's formidable Scout—or after a day of too much online shopping, I might relate to Edith Wharton's classic spendthrift, Lily Bart a bit more closely than I would like to. And during most of my twenties, Bridget Jones was my personal hero. But there was something about reading a *real* account of a young woman's early years in New York City that spoke directly to me. I understood the thrill that a new city brings, even if being lost on the subway or sharing your apartment with large flying insects are part of the equation. Cantwell writes of her first New York City apartment with an elegance that has made her memoir a classic:

> "The furniture—two studio couches, a big table, a couple of hard chairs, and a pier glass leaning against the fireplace—belongs to the landlord. We have our reading lamps from college, though, and Allies's phonograph, and ironing board and iron from S. Klein's on Union Square, some pots and pans, a small bottle of vermouth, and a fifth of Dixie Belle Gin. We have, in short, everything we need, anyway. There are nights when, cross-legged on my studio couch, Vivaldi's Four Seasons on the phonograph and stray cats scrabbling in the weeds outside the kitchen window, I can feel joy exploding in my chest."

That paragraph perfectly captures the promise of adventure, a woman's life unfolding—something big starting from almost nothing, and in a way, this is really what writing a memoir is all about. There are too many memoirs to count that have started from small stories—a child ignored but somehow growing up strong and successful; a woman losing herself in her marriage but choosing to cast her grief aside and take a long, healing trip; a boy in the projects of Red Hook who believed God was "the color of water." And another boy, this one in Ireland, whose house was flooded—but never mind, his family just pretended they lived in Venice. Could the authors of *The Glass Castle*; *Eat, Pray, Love*; *The Color of Water*; and *Angela's*

Ashes ever imagined that these singular details of their lives would eventually be turned into stories that would be read by millions of people around the world? And while the aforementioned memoirs are wonderful, there are many memoirs that are equally riveting but aren't exactly household names. I sincerely hope that this book will inspire you to experiment and read a few that you might not be familiar with.

Since reading Mary Cantwell's story, I've been delighted to learn that the world is full of wonderful storytellers—and as you probably know, there is a memoir to be found on almost every topic. Since most of us can't just go off to Italy or India for a year, or easily quit our jobs to try culinary school, sometimes reading a good memoir on the topic is the next best thing. And while I've always been curious about the goings-on in restaurant kitchens and culinary school greatly interests me, I know I'm much better off—and a lot safer—cooking in my own kitchen, so memoirs are the perfect stand-in. Then there are the memoirs where I'm so incredibly grateful I haven't had the same experience—*The Glass Castle, Angela's Ashes, Blackbird*—these are the memoirs that make me hug my family closer at night and nearly burst with gratitude over having something as simple as a hug from my young daughter. Memoirs are powerful and full of feeling, and they stick with you unlike books from any other genre.

The very fact that you're reading this book suggests that you, too, are a lover of other people's stories and, like me, have a relentless fascination with the lives of other people. You can't help but wonder what kinds of apartments people on the bus are going home to, or why it is the man in line next to you at the grocery store is buying flowers. Is he proposing? Did he have a fight with his wife? Or does he just like the way flowers look in his dining room? You find the smallest of details fascinating and nothing escapes you. Memoir lovers are a nosy lot, and wonderful tales are often spun from the smallest of details, which is probably why I've never stopped reading memoirs since the day I stumbled upon *Manhattan, When I Was Young.*

So what is the story you want to tell? Are you just a natural story-teller who can put an amusing spin on any tale and can keep everyone on the edge of their seats? Have you led an unusually challenging or extraordinary life and need some help getting it down on paper? Do you want to preserve your memories for generations to come? Are you planning to spend a year trekking through the rainforest and want to chronicle the experience? Whatever your story, the good news is that, while memoir writing can be incredibly challenging and daunting, it is possible to make the process a little easier with some proper planning and hard work. This book will walk you through the process by giving you some insight as to what has made some of the most successful memoirs of late appeal to millions of readers, and how you, too, can learn from them. I'll help you figure out what your strengths are as a memoir writer, what pieces of your story might best be left "in the drawer," what your "hook" is—that special something that makes your story different from everyone else's—and how to keep your life story from wandering and getting completely out of control. We'll work on all of the basics too—voice, dialogue, pacing, structure. Don't get me wrong, setting out to write a memoir is hard work, but by committing to this process and following these guidelines, you'll come out with a piece of writing you'll be proud of, and that will preserve the story you want to tell for generations to come.

preparing to write

I hate reading directions. I'm more of a dive right in and see if I can figure things out on my own kind of girl. I'll take this confession one step further and tell you that in my foolish past I've been known to skip an introduction when reading books such as this one. But luckily I've learned a thing or two over the years ... namely that if the author of a book that's proposing to teach you how to write and sell your memoir has bothered to include an introduction there's probably a good reason. I'd like to think that's the case here (read: if you skipped it, go back and read it!). I'm hoping that the introduction inspired you to get excited about the genre. Did it give you a "Hey yeah! That's exactly what I'm aiming to write!" sort of feeling? Good—if it did, then I succeeded. Writing a memoir is a big project, and you'll need to let that enthusiasm carry you through—while your memoir is coming along well, and also when you're feeling stuck and on the verge of giving up the entire endeavor all together. Trust me, it happens.

And if you *are* anything like me, right now you're feeling like you just want to jump up and get going already. You want to *write*! I'm here to ask you to think about a few things before you jump into the wild world that is memoir writing. What if I told you that by just reading these first few chapters and sorting through a few essential issues you could make your story more marketable? Hint: Publishers *love* marketable. What if by sitting back and listening to what I have to say you could learn how to boil your story down into a few essential talking points? Basically show you how to make your story all the more appealing to agents, editors, and media outlets? Handy information, people! Would you still want to jump in and start working on your own? Or would you be willing to listen? What if by starting out slowly I could save you the trouble of hearing the dreaded "sorry, we've already published ten memoirs about women who have quit their corporate jobs to make organic jam for a living." That's painful to hear after pounding out 300 pages of prose—believe me. But you wouldn't have had this problem if you'd read section one first! And lastly, I can help you sort out all of your memories so that you'll know exactly how to choose the ones that are the most interesting—and avoid the ones that are likely to bore a potential agent to death. Again, while I'm really not much of a fan of getting ready to do anything, I promise you it's worth it. So let's get READY TO WRITE.

CHAPTER ONE:

Understanding the Genre

T ruth is stranger than fiction. We've all heard this a million times before. But there is perhaps no better proof to this statement than the overwhelming success of some recent memoirs, and the unbelievable growth this genre has experienced over the past few years. Frank McCourt's groundbreaking *Angela's Ashes* spent two years on *The New York Times* bestseller list, won a Pulitzer Prize and a National Book Critics Circle Award, and more recently, Elizabeth Gilbert's runaway bestseller and Oprah pick *Eat, Pray, Love* captured the hearts of women everywhere and currently boasts an astonishing five million copies in print. Memoir lovers have eaten up books on topics covering everything from bizarrely abusive childhoods (*Angela's Ashes Blackbird, The Glass Castle, Running With Scissors*), addiction (*A Million Little Pieces, Dry, Drinking: A Love Story, Beautiful Boy*), food (*Julie & Julia, Tender at the Bone*), grief (*The Year of Magical Thinking*), unmanageable dogs (*Marley & Me*) and have even shed collective tears during the last days of two different college professors (*Tuesdays With Morrie* and *The Last Lecture*). Memoirs have worked their way into the American mainstream and show no signs of turning back.

Memoir writers are a brave lot. It takes guts to tell a story—*your story*—so publicly. But memoir writers often find that the story they carry inside of them simply needs to be told, whether it means coming clean about an abusive childhood, or sharing a story about a life-changing trip. And what is the story that *you* need to tell? And why a memoir? There are many other formats in which to tell your story. Personal essays, magazine articles, blogs, and, of course, the local pub are all viable options. But a full-length memoir allows for exploration of the topic at hand, and provides an opportunity to use tension and pacing to draw the reader through your entire story. A memoir is the perfect canvas for a writer to relay an experience completely on her own terms, through her choice of setting, tone, style, voice, format—and even how she portrays her "characters" and uses dialogue. But before we start getting down to work on your memoir, it's important that we take a few moments to discuss those particular elements that make a memoir different from other literary formats. Having a better understanding of what's generally expected of this format is going to make the planning process easier, help you determine what are your strengths as a writer and how to highlight them, as well as figure out what are the strengths of your *story* and how to maximize them as you're planning out your memoir. There are so many different ways to write a memoir—an author isn't limited to a chronological retelling of events from point A to point B—so a closer look at some of the key elements is a must.

HOW MEMOIRS DIFFER FROM OTHER GENRES

KEY DIFFERENCE #1:
Memoirs Create a Personal Connection Between the Author and Reader

This is perhaps one of the greatest differences between memoirs, journalism, and fiction. There is no other genre (other than maybe the personal essay—but hey, it's an essay, there's only so far you can go) where the author is so closely connected to the reader. You can "fake it," of course, with novels; everyone has felt a close connection to fictional characters, and this can certainly be meaningful, but we all know that ultimately our beloved favorite characters aren't real. But knowing the individual whose story you are following is a real live person who did, in fact, experience and feel every emotion and event you are reading on the page is powerful.

While journalists often serve as a guide in narrative nonfiction, which can be a wonderful way to experience a place or event that we may never otherwise have a chance to see up close, journalists are of course impartial. A journalist's job is to investigate a particular topic and his objective isn't to tell you about his experience, but to collect and document the experiences of others. This is of course a good thing when it comes to journalism, but with memoir, the beauty is in experiencing the emotions, and expectations—both the good and bad—with the author, which just isn't possible with journalism. Another important aspect of the author/reader relationship however, is that this usually means that regardless of whatever horrific acts the memoirist may have committed, they must come across as likeable to the reader. This means that after a long and terrible career of say, slaying kittens, or stealing candy from small children, the memoirist must be self-reflective enough—must have learned enough from her experience that the reader can put such atrocities aside and look beyond the bad. If the person writing the memoir is waking up every morning and saying, "Hey, I'm going to see how big of a jerk I can be today! Watch me ruin lives!" it's likely that their story is just not going to have wide appeal. I will admit that there are a couple of notable exceptions to this rule, but such exceptions are rare, and you would be well advised to avoid this format if you do not have enough distance from your past actions to come across with any remorse.

KEY DIFFERENCE #2:

Memoirs Transport Readers to a Place They Wouldn't Ordinarily be Able to Go

Most memoirs are written (obviously) because the author has a story or experience that is worth sharing—or their experience has taken them to a place that ultimately provides a valuable lesson, one that is universal enough that a wide audience is going to glean value from it. This experience can range from anything from a bizarre or abusive childhood to an unusual job as a fisherman or maybe a magician. In recent years, we've seen memoirs on everything from living with dogs, living with cancer, surviving drugs and alcohol addiction, spending a year without shopping, and losing spouses to learning to cook French cuisine. A memoir takes readers to a place that they aren't ordinarily able to go, or frankly, wouldn't want to go on their own accord, and it's the memoirist job to re-create the experience for them in a satisfying way on the written page. This means that you must have a story that is "share worthy," and you must be able to successfully and accurately re-create your story with colorful description, vivid dialogue, and masterful storytelling.

KEY DIFFERENCE #3:

Memoirs Must Successfully Battle the "So What?" Moment

Bringing a story to life on the page is about more than just "having the material." A memoirist needs to be able to translate her story into a lively, engaging, and share worthy story that a reader is willing to plunk down his hard earned cash. Nearly every description of a memoir hits what I like to call the "so what? moment". If you take a second to think about it, most (not all mind you, but most) memoirs are not written under the most extraordinary circumstances. Because of this, the memoirist has to bring quite a few additional elements into the mix to make his story worth the fifteen to even thirty dollars it will cost you to buy it. Case in point: Most best-selling memoirs, if you were to boil the story down to their core, probably have the same story as someone who lives down the street from you, or as someone who works in your office. Chances are, you know a woman who went through a horrible divorce, a man who had terrible childhood, or even someone who has a really semi-cute but precocious dog. So what? Do you want to hear about their divorce or this dog every day? Let's take this a step further: Would you actually give them twenty-six dollars to read intimate details about their divorce or this mischievous dog? Chances are you would probably start to find this divorcée/dog incredibly annoying and dull, would go to great lengths to avoid this person, and would seriously consider giving them twenty-six dollars to never mention their divorce/ dog again. This is what I call the "so what?" moment. Since most of us are not princesses, daughters of famous rock stars, etc., we just don't automatically have the kind of mind-blowing material that results in the "tell me more" situation right off the bat. That doesn't mean we don't have the material to write a fascinating memoir—it just means we have to battle the "so what? moment" using some of the other tools in our toolbox. While we'll get into the specifics of how to do this in Part Two of the book, for now, you need to know that some of the weapons used for battling this problem are:

- voice
- format
- style
- universal themes
- relatability
- a good hook
- clean parameters
- an engaging moment of discovery

BEFORE YOU BEGIN . . .

As with most things in life, whether it is applying for college, buying a home, or interviewing for a job, it's generally advisable to approach the matter in a semi-knowledgeable fashion. Obviously, you tend to agree, since here you are, reading this book. As a member of the publishing industry, I'm constantly astonished when my colleagues tell me they just "don't have time to read." Um, what??!! I'm a firm believer that to break into any business, and in this case you've chosen the arguably eccentric and incredibly competitive business that is memoir writing, it's best you know who and what you're up against. Trying to write a memoir without knowing a) what is considered the best of the best, b) knowing what the different types of memoirs out there "feel like," and c) not being familiar enough with the genre to toss around the most popular titles and their authors and publisher's names with ease would be doing yourself a huge disservice. I'm not suggesting that you need to take a leave of absence from work and spend a year reading every memoir that was published. But I am suggesting that maybe you find a way to carve out some extra time every day to devote some time to research. This might mean getting up a half hour early every morning to read, turning off the television, or not going to the movies. Do whatever you need to do to find some extra reading time. Chances are, if you're feeling the bug to actually write a memoir, you'll find the reading immensely enjoyable.

A Couple of Rules to Remember

Whether your goal is to write the next *Autobiography of a Face* or *The Middle Place* after a difficult illness, or simply use your witty storytelling abilities to put a fresh spin on what law school is really like, you have that option, because one of the best things about memoir writing is how much freedom there is for experimentation.

There is always room for a fresh new voice, or an author who knows how to make a story work within an exciting new format. But, there are a couple of simple rules it would be wise to follow closely.

1. Memoirs vs. Autobiographies: Do Not Write a Single Word Until You Understand the Difference

Unless you are Bill Clinton or Eleanor Roosevelt (in which case you have resurrected yourself from the dead, which in itself would make for a fascinating memoir) or some other equally important person of significant historical stature, *you are not writing an autobiography.* There seems to be much confusion on this topic, and as a lover of memoirs, I can't help but think the world will be a better place once this issue has been sorted out once and for all. An autobiography is a biography written by the person who is in fact also the subject of the book. In other words, an autobiography is the entire life story of a particular individual. Still not following me? The more you familiarize yourself with the genre, the more you'll see what I'm talking about—I swear. Traditionally, autobiographies are reserved for individuals who are extraordinarily famous, since an autobiography literally spans an individual's entire life, and, in fact, usually talks about the previous couple of generations of their families. A regular Joe just isn't going to be interesting enough to warrant that in-depth look at his life. Princess Diana wrote an autobiography, and I assure you that she was famous enough—even at such a young age—to warrant such a thorough treatment of her life story. I'm certain her fans would want to know every detail of her life, including information about her parents and siblings. If I were to write an autobiography (don't worry Mom and Dad, I have no plans to!), I assure you that no one could possibly care less as to whether or not it was snowing on the day I was born. As for Princess Di, surely there are chat groups devoted to that very topic. Are you starting to see the difference?

To date, memoir has come to mean an autobiographical work that is generally more specific in nature or that encapsulates a specific period of time or an experience. In other words, your memoir *does not need to cover every detail of your entire life.* Trust me, no publisher or agent wants to get a query letter for a memoir that begins with, "It was raining the day I was born." It's never a good sign. It generally means that there are 850, 10-point font, single-spaced manuscript pages to follow. If you start to pay attention to the timeframe of the memoirs you're reading, you'll note that they tend to cover a fairly specific period. So, a memoir is not so much a "life story" as it is a "story of a life experience." If you're not sure how to whittle back your life story into a manageable section, we'll talk about that more in chapter three. For now, just keep in mind that this is not going to be a day-by-day, week-by-week, play-by-play of *your* life.

2. A Memoir Is Not a Book-Length Rant

While writing is certainly a cathartic exercise, you would be wise not to confuse anger with passion. A memoir is not the place to air your frustrations with your ex-wife, your place of employment, your jerk next-door neighbor, or anything else that's angering you for that matter. While frustrations, emotions, depression—all sorts of unpleasantness—come up when writing a memoir, they must be part of some sort of greater theme, lest your memoir come out as one large e-mail to the universe's complaint department. Who would want to read that? (Hello! Go buy a journal!) Just keep in mind that your own personal anger regarding a specific issue isn't necessarily enough material for a full-length work. You must have learned from your experience and be able to communicate what was going on in your situation in a way that will make sense to readers on some sort of universal level so that they are able to connect with you.

ROUNDUP OF ALL-STAR MEMOIRS

It's impossible to predict which books will become massive best-sellers—believe me, if anyone ever managed to solve that puzzle, the publishing industry would be able to pay much better salaries! And while I would never recommend modeling your own project directly after an already published book, it is certainly possible to draw inspiration from past successes. I'm a big fan of reading and rereading well received books that may be similar in theme to your own book with an eye for elements that may prove helpful. Keep paper and a pencil handy and be ready to note anything that might inspire you. You might find yourself thinking, "It's really cool how this author breaks down her marriage into three different sections. That wouldn't work for my book about raising children—but it might be an interesting way to revisit the way I handle this section about watching my parents grow older." Inspiration can come from anywhere. It's about being willing and able to recognize it when the opportunity is presented to you.

Since you are almost ready to start writing your own memoir, keep the following concepts in mind as you add new memoirs to your library or reread old favorites:

- interesting ideas about how to handle structure
- how different authors use flashback and move through time
- where and why different memoirs begin and end when they do
- how authors highlight sections where they seem to have "revelations"
- how authors use dialogue to add color to their stories
- what you like about each memoir
- what you don't like about each memoir

Okay, I'm sure you've already figured out that I'm a very passionate memoir reader. I really eat them up. However, what you probably don't know is that I'm actual very skeptical when it comes to memoirs. I tend to be a sucker for the underdog memoir. If I haven't heard of it, chances are I'll want to read it. So when everyone and their mother (and, of course, Oprah) are positively swooning over a memoir, I'm actually a pretty tough customer. But I was pleasantly surprised when I reread these mega-hits. These memoirs are all wildly successful for a reason, and it's definitely worth taking a closer look at their strengths to try to glean what might have made them resonate with readers. Naturally there are quite a few memoirs out there that have reached superstar status, and while I couldn't possibly cover them all, I have included a list of memoirs that have spent a significant amount of time on *The New York Times* best-seller list.

REALITY CHECK: *You might be thinking, "If these memoirs are so successful, shouldn't I just write one exactly like it, except a little different? Like a male version of* Eat, Pray, Love?" *NO! The examples I give are meant to inspire—not to be copied. Originality is key in publishing; rehashing someone else's material will get you nowhere.*

EAT, PRAY, LOVE BY ELIZABETH GILBERT

BASIC PREMISE

A thirtysomething woman who seemed to have it all (husband, career, country house, apartment in New York City) is left feeling confused, trapped, overwhelmed, and most of all, terrified to have a child. She finds herself crying in a panic on her bathroom floor one night, doing something that she can only liken to praying, when she hears an oddly comforting godlike voice say "go back to bed Liz." This experience is soon followed by a divorce that can only be described as one for the record books, and the depression that came along with it was equally awful. Gilbert then decides to take an epic trip to explore three natures of herself in three different locations. She travels to Italy to eat, Bali to pray, and Indonesia to love.

A TYPICAL MOMENT

> *At the beginning of my spiritual experiment, I didn't always have such faith in this internal voice of wisdom. I remember once reaching for my private notebook in a bitter fury of rage and sorrow, and scrawling a message to my inner voice—to my divine interior comfort—that took up an entire page of capital letters: "I DO NOT FUCKING BELIEVE IN YOU!!!" After a moment, still breathing heavily, I felt a clear pinpoint of light ignite within me, and then I found myself writing this amused and ever-calm reply. Who are you talking to, then?*

WHY IT WORKS: THE BREAKDOWN

1. *Eat, Pray, Love* has an interesting format. The book is structured exactly like a japa malas prayer bead (note to reader—if you're ever confused about structure, apparently you can look anywhere for inspiration!). Her story, like her beads, are broken down into 108 tales, and into three sections (Eat, Pray, and Love)—which she also points out is the same as the holy trinity. Pretty interesting right off the bat. You immediately get the feeling that this isn't just an ordinary tale of woe of some woman's divorce.

2. Who hasn't been heartbroken, depressed, completely lost, and felt like a loser? It would be easy to instantly dislike a woman who gets to run around the world eating pasta and doing yoga for a year, but as she shares her experiences, she does so in such a way that you think, "Yeah, I've been there." She is a "relatable character." And a likeable one, too. She picks herself up and takes control of her life. She's every heartbroken woman's hero.

3. She manages to be serious and funny at the same time, and how she manages to do this on the topic of spirituality, is something of a marvel. It would be very easy to sound smug after doing several hours of silent meditation, but she still

manages to inject the perfect amount of self-deprecation. She wants the reader to understand that she takes both her happiness and her spirituality very seriously, but she also wants you to know that she fully intends to continue to be a regular person, and that her previous few months of eating gelato and pasta are an important part of her personality, too. And notice the setting of her first epiphany. It isn't an ancient church, a beautiful fountain, or even a romantic café; it's her bathroom floor. Nothing says grounded like having an epiphany on the floor of your bathroom.

4. She listens and asks the right questions. I think this is an important point, and ultimately where a lot of her humor comes from. I noticed that most of the sections in *Eat, Pray, Love* that made me laugh were based on her observations of others. Case in point: Her sister's explanation of what it's like to have a baby, which she describes as "like getting a tattoo on your face. You have to make sure you really want it." If she wasn't listening, but just blathering on about her own grief, she would have missed this, and her memoir would be missing a lot of its richness and color as a result. She also asks questions of herself that many women just don't bother to ask. "What do you want to do Liz?" "What would you find enjoyable to do today Liz?" Is it possible that she's just found a way to make her grief much more glamorous and, therefore, more fun to read about than the average woman's? Entirely possible, but definitely something every memoir writer can learn from.

ANGELA'S ASHES BY FRANK MCCOURT

BASIC PREMISE

Frank McCourt chronicles his self-described "miserable Irish Catholic childhood"—and, as he states, "the happy childhood is hardly worth your while." When McCourt starts off by saying his childhood was miserable, he means it. The story you go on to read is so unbelievably miserable, you keep soldiering on, certain that their lot is just about to change. The children are at the complete mercy of their parents, who are at complete odds with each other about how to go about providing for children. It's a bleak picture for sure. There's no food, no work, and as McCourt points out, *they are always wet*. But this story is nevertheless captivating, and not just in a car wreck waiting to happen kind of way. There is a sense that the God this incredibly Catholic family is praying to every single Sunday surely will not let this suffering go on much longer. There are hints of love, some high points, and ultimately, McCourt himself is so charming and tenacious that you can't stop reading.

A TYPICAL MOMENT

> *I don't know why we can't keep Eugene. I don't know why they have to send him away with that man who puts his pint on the white coffin. I don't know why they had to send Margaret away and Oliver. It is a bad thing to put my sister and my brothers in a box and I wish I could say something to someone.*

WHY IT WORKS: THE BREAKDOWN

1. McCourt has an interesting approach to telling his own story. He manages to convey the facts in a manner that isn't overly emotional—he has just enough distance from the story to make it readable. Were the tragic events of *Angela's Ashes* told from the mother's point of view for instance, this memoir may have simply been too sad to read. This may have something to do with the fact that we're seeing the events through McCourt's eyes as a young boy. His narration presents a naiveté that certainly gets across the seriousness and sadness of their situation, but also offers the reader a bit of protection.

2. While this may be one of the most horrific accounts of childhood gone wrong, there is not an ounce of bitterness to be found anywhere in McCourt's memoir. When journalist John McGuire asked him about this in an interview for the *St. Louis Post-Dispatch*, he responded: "Oh, it would be like having some deep bitterness over a bad storm that hit Limerick.

Nobody understands an act of God." There isn't anything much more inspiring than that. I'm still angry that I missed the UPS guy today!

3. His prose is reminiscent of the Irish storytelling tradition, and I think it's best summed up by Malcolm Jones who covered one of McCourt's tours for *Newsweek* and also wrote the following in the same magazine shortly after his death:

> Reduced to its essentials, Angela's Ashes *looks like an encyclopedia of Irish cliché—the alcoholic pa, the long-suffering ma, the wee lads without a crust among 'em. Yet somehow McCourt sidesteps sentimentality with a litany of hardship that would make a cynic flinch. "My father and mother should have stayed in New York where they met and married and where I was born," the book begins. By the time the family moved back to Ireland in 1934, four-year-old Frank had gained three brothers and lost a sister. Two more brothers would be born, and two would die. The father drank his paycheck and eventually wandered off for good during World War II. The mother, the Angela of the title, begged for charity and lived off the mingy help of relatives, at one point sleeping with a cousin so that her children might have a place to live. People who haven't read the book always ask, "Isn't it awfully depressing?" Yes, but it's also awfully funny. The genius of the book is that the tears and laughter are rarely separated by so much as a comma.*

THE COLOR OF WATER BY JAMES MCBRIDE

BASIC PREMISE

A young man, who is also a writer and a musician, had always been puzzled by his racial identity, so he decides to clarify it for once and for all by researching his mysterious and somewhat dark family history. His mother, Ruth McBride Jordan, concealed her identity as the daughter of an Orthodox Jewish rabbi after she married a black man. She moved to Harlem, converted to Christianity, and even helped to cofound a Baptist congregation. She is twice widowed by men she loved, yet manages to raise twelve extraordinary children in the projects of Red Hook, Brooklyn.

A TYPICAL MOMENT

> C'mon," she said, "I'll walk you to the bus stop." Surprise
> reward. Me and Mommy alone. It was the first time I re-
> member ever being alone with my mother. It became the
> high point of my day, a memory so sweet it is burned into
> my mind like a tattoo, Mommy walking me to the bus stop
> and every afternoon picking me up. . .

WHY IT WORKS: THE BREAKDOWN

1. The format—the story is told in alternating voices, both James McBride's and his mother Ruth McBride's. Since they are coming at the story from different viewpoints, and with different styles, this approach keeps the prose lively and engaging. I found myself anxious to get back to both of their stories and hungry for more, as they both added a lot to the story.

2. It is genuinely inspiring. The hardships the McBrides experienced are intense—yet this memoir is full of love, passion, intelligence, and success. Ruth's achievements with her children do not come across in a Lifetime Movie/Hallmark Hall of Fame sort of way—but through a simplicity and determination that is refreshing and impossible not to be moved by. How can you not be affected by a child whose greatest joy is that he gets to be alone with his mother for a few precious moments at the bus stop every day? McBride's observations about being part of a large and poor family aren't always positive and pretty, but every so often, they are so lovely that their hardships come across as just an unfortunate side effect.

3. In addition to providing a great story, this memoir moves through all sorts of places and time—Brooklyn during different time periods, Harlem, the Deep South, Manhattan—and McBride has the skill to move through different time periods with ease.

THE YEAR OF MAGICAL THINKING BY JOAN DIDION

BASIC PREMISE

Joan Didion and her husband, John Dunne, also a writer, enjoyed a long and happy marriage. As Didion puts it "there was no separation between our investments or our interests in any given situation." After visiting their only daughter, who was in the intensive care unit at a nearby hospital, her husband suffered a fatal heart attack as they were about to have dinner. *The Year of Magical Thinking* is an exploration of grief. It presents an in-depth and most unusual look at what the grieving process is like for someone who is experiencing it firsthand.

A TYPICAL MOMENT

> *I see how that my insistence on spending that first night alone was more complicated than it seemed, a primitive instinct. Of course I knew John was dead. Of course I had already delivered the definitive news to his brother and to my brother and to Quintana's husband. The New York Times knew. Yet I was myself in no way prepared to accept this news as final: There was a level on which I believed that what had happened remained reversible. That was why I needed to be alone.*

WHY IT WORKS: THE BREAKDOWN

1. Didion is oddly able to look at her own grieving through a very unusual set of lenses—that of both a journalist and a grieving widow. She's able to see that much of her behavior was irrational—yet self-aware enough to understand that she could not realize at the time just how irrational she actually was.

2. As a skilled journalist, she looks at grieving from a different perspective. This isn't just a compilation of research—facts from experts on the topic, interviews, etc. Didion is able to ask the right questions, like "Why was she able to immediately authorize an autopsy but not organ donation?" She is aware that there is meaning in the smallest of gestures and the oddest of reactions. She is able to see that her ability to give away her husband's clothes but not his shoes (when he comes back, he'll obviously need shoes is her rationale) are ultimately examples or her total inability to think rationally during this period. She believes this is due to the fact that deep down, on some level, part of her believes her actions

have the power to change the outcome of what happened to her husband.

3. While she does sometimes come off as a "cool customer," you really come to see that this reaction is just honestly how humans work. As you move further along in the book, you really see that it's also a love story and a memorial to a family as well.

AUTOBIOGRAPHY OF A FACE BY LUCY GREALY

BASIC PREMISE

Grealy was diagnosed with a rare form of cancer at the age of nine, which left her disfigured and subjected her to a life that included physical and emotional pain and included an extraordinary number of surgeries. Growing up with a disfigured face during a time when beauty is revered caused Grealy to internalize all her fears of being rejected and unloved.

A TYPICAL MOMENT

> When a film's heroine innocently coughs, you know that two scenes later, at most, she'll be in an oxygen tent; when a man bumps into a woman at the train station, you know that man will become the woman's lover and/or murderer. In everyday life, where we cough often and are always bumping into people, our daily actions rarely reverberate so lucidly. Once we love or hate someone, we can think back and remember that first casual encounter. But what of all the chance meetings that nothing ever comes of? While our bodies move ever forward on the time line, our minds continuously trace backward, seeking shape and meaning as deftly as any arrow seeking its mark.

WHY IT WORKS: THE BREAKDOWN

1. Lucy Grealy was a poet, and every line of *Autobiography of a Face* is beautiful, which is amazing, since a good portion of this book takes place in a children's cancer ward. Because of her skills as a poet, she is able to communicate her emotions clearly, and her observations are interesting,

sharp, and emotional, but never overly sentimental. She never takes cheap shots, and this memoir makes you think.

2. Her observations on beauty and self-consciousness manage to feel universal even though they obviously spring from her personal situation.

> I was my face, I was ugliness—though sometimes unbearable, also offered a possible point of escape. It became the launching pad from which to lift off, the one immediately recognizable place to point to when asked what was wrong with my life. Everything led to it, everything receded from it—my face as personal vanishing point.

While thankfully most people don't have to suffer though thirty-plus surgeries like Lucy Grealy (and if you're not familiar with Grealy, she sadly died of an accidental drug overdose at the age of thirty-nine), I think it's safe to say that most of us, at one time or another, have been tempted to transfer the blame to some of life's problems to our appearances. This is a universal feeling, and Grealy articulated it perfectly.

3. She manages to be self-aware. Toward the end of her memoir, she confesses to "trying enlightenment" and failing. She goes through a period of understanding that chemo wasn't meant to be "her punishment" and that maybe her face was hers to serve a higher purpose. But then later on when a bone graft is reabsorbed and her face doesn't take on the more "normal" appearance she hopes it will, she suffers another letdown. *Autobiography of a Face* is real. If this memoir was neatly tied up with a positive ending, I think it might be hard to buy. The author makes great strides and has setbacks—it's real life.

THE GLASS CASTLE BY JEANNETTE WALLS

BASIC PREMISE
The author, a successful journalist, decided to tell her story of growing up in extreme poverty and with parents who had very un-

usual ideas about how to raise their four children after she saw her homeless mother digging for food in a dumpster while sitting in a taxi on the way to an industry event. Walls' childhood was marked by deprivation, neglect, and the further decline of their family as her parents put their own false hopes and dreams before the needs of their children. The family eventually ends up in a West Virginia mining town, but miraculously, Walls and two of her siblings manage to escape that lifestyle and make their way to New York City.

A TYPICAL MOMENT

> *Dad came home in the middle of the night a few months later and roused all of us from bed. "Time to pull up the stakes and leave this shit-hole behind," he hollered. We had fifteen minutes to gather whatever we needed and pile into the car. "Is everything okay, Dad?" I asked. "Is someone after us?" "Don't you worry," Dad said. "You leave that to me. Don't I always take care of you?" "'Course you do," I said. "That's my girl!" Dad said with a hug, then barked orders at us all to speed things up. He took the essentials—a big black cast-iron skillet and the Dutch oven, some army-surplus tin plates, a few knives, his pistol, and Mom's archery set—and packed them in the trunk of the Blue Goose. He said we shouldn't take much else, just what we needed to survive. Mom hurried out to the yard and started digging holes by the light of the moon, looking for our jar of cash. She had forgotten where she'd buried it.*

WHY IT WORKS: THE BREAKDOWN

1. While I wouldn't wish neglectful parents of any sort on anyone, Walls' parents are certainly more interesting than your typical neglectful parents. They present a curious combination of "street smarts"—or whatever you would call the kind of smarts that allow you to survive in the desert—and an appreciation for art and intellect, but they also completely lack any sort of understanding of the basic needs of children. It's not that they come across as completely unloving, but as if they're missing one big piece of the parenting puzzle.

2. The parents' larger-than-life stories give this memoir an almost mythological feel. Everything the parents set out to do

promises to be grand and tremendously exciting. Nothing is normal in this family. The story of how Walls' parents met is a perfect example. Everything about this story screams "tall tale." Walls' mother walks up to a group of Air Force men who are afraid to dive off a cliff. She does a perfect swan dive. Her father decides to jump in after her as, "No way in hell, he'd say, was he letting a fine broad like that get away from him." And he proceeds to do a "parachute dive without a parachute." The story goes on that he told her he would marry her, but twenty-three men had already proposed. She finally agreed as he "wouldn't take no for an answer." Everything about this couple is exaggerated and dramatic, which may not make for good parenting, but does make for good reading.

3. I wouldn't say *The Glass Castle* is about a particularly loving family, but there are times when you can't help but get swept up in their dynamic. There are situations that would scar a normal person for life—both the child and the parent—that simply become another hilarious episode in this memoir. When the author actually falls out of her family's moving car as a very young girl and is injured as she rolls down an embankment, left there to wonder if her family is ever coming back for her, her father's comment, when they finally do come back for her is "Damn, honey, you busted your snot locker pretty good." The author describes how she told her siblings and mother about the word "snot locker" and how they all thought it was as hilarious as she did." Just another funny moment in the Walls family.

HOMEWORK

1. Read or Refamiliarize Yourself With Best-Selling Memoirs

Ask yourself what makes these memoirs favorites of yours. Is it the voice? The structure? The way you connect to the author? Why do you think these particular memoirs had such a huge impact on a large readership? If one of these hit memoirs just isn't your cup of tea (which is totally okay by the way, you can't like everything), why not? What doesn't work for you?

2. Bigger Isn't Always Better

Some of my favorite memoirs are not huge bestsellers. Ask for recommendations from friends, booksellers, or librarians. (Librarians are in fact my favorite source for book recommendations. They can recommend truly based on their gut, as they don't have to worry about selling books). Read these memoirs simply for pleasure and enjoyment, but with an eye for inspiration. What do you like about these works, and how do they inspire you?

3. Consider Joining or Starting a Memoir Reading Group

Since it can be difficult to carve out time for reading, yet it remains essential to your work to keep up to date on the memoirs that are in the marketplace, think about participating in a memoir-only reading group. The deadline of the meeting will keep you focused, and it can be helpful to hear other thoughts and opinions while you're working on a particular project. This would also be a great way to learn about other memoirs that you may not have heard of before.

> **REALITY CHECK**: *If you're thinking, "Hey, the only story I'm really interested in is* mine, *I just can't be bothered to read anyone else's," I urge you to reconsider. While writing your memoir obviously involves spending quite a bit of timed focused on the details of* your *life, don't make the mistake of thinking that other writers and their stories don't have something to offer you. You'll be doing yourself a major disservice if you allow your ego to drive the entire project, and trust me, your work will suffer as a result.*

4. Start Jogging Down Memory Lane

Memoirs are obviously all about memories, so get prepared to start digging through the past. Whether you are writing about something from your childhood or an upcoming trip to the rain forest, your past is going to come into play, as a memoir is ultimately the story of *who* you are and how you came to be the person who is doing something crazy like sleeping in the Amazon without a tent for six months. So don't fool yourself into thinking your past doesn't matter. Spend some time sifting through photo albums, old letters, journals, mementos, whatever you have that might prove meaningful. While I'm not suggesting you need to go wild cataloging every moment of your life from birth on, it may be helpful to have reasonable and organized access to items from your past. Take notes about what you find. You very well may find that a photograph will lead you to other things. It might remind you of a place you hadn't thought of in years, a friend you'd like to reach out to, and so forth. Many of these paths may prove helpful in the writing of your memoir, so keep careful track of where these thoughts take you.

RECOMMENDED READING

Following is a list of best-selling and critically acclaimed memoirs to get you started. I did my best to include as many titles as I could, but it was impossible to cover them all. There is also suggested reading in the other chapters that talk about voice, structure, etc., and some of those big blockbuster memoirs that are a particularly fine example of "voice" might be listed there as well. Basically, if you choose to read some of the memoirs in the suggested reading section of this chapter, you'll find you've already done a good portion of the suggested reading for the other chapters. I'm always on the lookout for a great memoir recommendation, as I positively hate the idea of missing out on a good one! So please let me know if you find a must-read memoir that I haven't listed. Please feel free to e-mail any great finds to paula@morningmemoir.com. Also, I've asked many of the memoirists whose books I've mentioned to share the title of their favorite memoir and to let us know what it is about that title that inspired them. You'll see their favorites mentioned throughout the book.

BEST-SELLING AND CRITICALLY ACCLAIMED MEMOIRS

Angela's Ashes by Frank McCourt

The Glass Castle by Jeannette Walls

The Tender Bar by J.R. Moehringer

Manhattan, When I Was Young by Mary Cantwell

Speaking With Strangers by Mary Cantwell

The Year of Magical Thinking by Joan Didion

The Color of Water by James McBride

Night by Elie Wiesel

Drinking: A Love Story by Caroline Knapp

Marley & Me by John Grogan

Autobiography of a Face by Lucy Grealy

The Liars' Club by Mary Karr

Cherry by Mary Karr

A Girl Named Zippy by Haven Kimmel

Tender at the Bone by Ruth Reichl

Comfort Me With Apples by Ruth Reichl

Dreams From My Father by Barack Obama

Eat, Pray, Love by Elizabeth Gilbert

Running With Scissors by Augusten Burroughs

Dry by Augusten Burroughs

CHAPTER TWO:

What's Your Hook?

ithin a month of signing my appointment papers to become an assistant professor of psychiatry at the University of California, Los Angeles, I was well on my way to madness.

—KAY REDFIELD JAMISON, author of *An Unquiet Mind*

Kay Redfield Jamison is both a professor of psychiatry at Johns Hopkins University School of Medicine and suffers from severe manic-depressive illness herself. She writes about her struggles with the disease as she's starting out her medical career in her best-selling memoir *An Unquiet Mind*. A mentally ill psychiatrist: This is what's known in publishing as "the hook." A hook is that certain something that makes your book marketable. It's an element that is utterly unique to your story. It is memorable, compelling, sometimes controversial, and appealing to the media. Jamison's hook is poetic and ironic, while others may be tragic, inspiring, shocking, funny—or may feature a special setting, show off someone's unusual ability, or demonstrate survival against all odds. Your hook is going to capture the reader's attention and enable you to lure her in, but it is your job as a writer to keep her captured with your story and your writing style.

While not every memoirist can be the sole survivor of an airplane crash, a popular 1970s child star, or a mafia princess, fear not, this doesn't mean your story doesn't have a hook. A hook isn't necessarily about surviving an ill-fated climb on Mount Everest or spending a year traveling around the French countryside on a bicycle. Finding your hook is about presenting your story in a marketable and interesting fashion that best displays your skills and strengths as a writer.

A DIVORCE IS A DIVORCE AND IS *STILL* A DIVORCE. . .

While a good hook can give fresh energy and put a new spin on a topic that may seem familiar, it is important to note that the underlying theme of your memoir and your hook are not necessarily the same thing. While the distinction between the two can be subtle, a clear understanding of them can make the difference between writing "just another divorce memoir" and the next *Eat, Pray, Love*. The key here is learning to tune in to those tiny clues, honing in on the unique set of details that make your divorce memoir, love story, life with an autistic child, or career change memoir different from everyone else's, but at the same time managing to capture that universal feeling that people in similar circumstances experience. This magical combination results in a story that is both new and relatable at the same time. In other words, the hook takes things a step further by building elements onto your theme that are meaningful to you and you alone, but still appealing to readers interested in your topic. Be sure to keep the following key points in mind as we take a closer look at the hooks and themes of some popular memoirs to see how some authors use a hook to play up common themes such as divorce, travel, food, spirituality, and survival.

The Good Hook Checklist

- A good hook brings something new to the table.
- A hook goes beyond the theme of the memoir.
- A hook can be summed up in a sentence or two.

- The right hook is provocative and memorable.
- A hook can be described with three key words.

A ROUNDUP OF GOOD HOOKS

Now that we're all clear on the elements of a good hook, let's take a closer look at what makes up the hook in some recent memoirs. Remember, it takes some practice, but soon you should be spotting a good hook for a book in no time at all.

EAT, PRAY, LOVE BY ELIZABETH GILBERT

THEMES: Divorce, Travel, Spirituality, Food

THE HOOK: After a painful divorce, the author sets out to find the opposite of what she's feeling by devoting one year specifically to pleasure, prayer, and love. She travels to three distinctly different locales to immerse herself in these pursuits. Can a heartbroken and confused woman purposely set out to find pleasure, peace, and even love?

WHAT'S UNUSUAL ABOUT IT?: She's taking the reader along on her quest to heal, and she doesn't have a clue what's going to happen. She's going about her healing in an unexpected way and with the three portions of her quest being somewhat contrary. She's also deciding that she wants to feel happy, and is constructing a trip solely with that end in mind, which is the opposite approach of similar memoirs such as *An Italian Affair* and *Under the Tuscan Sun*.

CHERRIES IN WINTER BY SUZAN COLON

THEMES: Family, Food, Hard Times, Inspiration

THE HOOK: After losing a high-powered and glamorous job at a magazine, the author realized she had to cut way back when it came to spending money. Her mother suggested that she look through her grandmother's file for some money-saving recipe ideas, which led to a discovery that was more helpful than just a

---

stash of recipes for clam chowder and beef stew. Colon soon realized that in addition to recipes for comfort food, she had also stumbled upon her family's "recipe" for surviving hard times.

WHAT'S UNUSUAL ABOUT IT?: Rather than plunging into "woe is me" mode about how she can no longer afford designer shoes and handbags, this magazine editor decides to take action and plunge directly into a sweet (both figuratively and literally) and moving family history.

AUTOBIOGRAPHY OF A FACE BY LUCY GREALY

THEMES: Illness, Survival

THE HOOK: The author spent many years of her life, from early childhood on being treated for a rare form of cancer that left her disfigured. In addition to physical recovery, Grealy's rich and complicated fantasy life helped her with an even more difficult emotional recovery that she brilliantly chronicles in her highly regarded memoir.

WHAT'S UNUSUAL ABOUT IT?: This isn't simply an "I conquered cancer" story, but a complicated tale of coming to terms with appearance in a time where beauty counts for everything. Grealy's story of learning that beauty comes from within borders on heroic.

These are just three examples of memoirs where a common, ordinary situation is brought to life by sparkling details. It is also important to note that these authors, like other successful memoirists, managed to avoid common pitfalls that can make the most riveting story painful to read. We'll talk more about voice in chapter five, but keep in mind that no one wants to read a book-length rant about how much you hate your job, or a bitter tale of a marriage gone wrong. These hooks are also clear. Once you understand what they are, they are carefully executed throughout the entirety of the memoir. They don't flow off in a million different directions, nor do they stop midway, leaving the reader without any closure. Be sure to avoid the following pitfalls when working out your hook.

Common Hook Pitfalls

- Mistaking bitterness or anger for passion—it's not a reason to write a book.
- A hook that isn't relatable to readers.
- A hook that takes too long to build or starts too late in the story.
- A hook that is too complicated or follows too many different paths.
- A hook that doesn't follow through to the end of the story.

Hooks of All Kinds— Where Does Your Story Fall?

While most memoirs tend to fall into one of the following categories, I dare say it's possible that every once in a blue moon, you'll encounter one that, (gasp!), just might fall somewhere outside the general parameters of what I'm outlining below. If you find your memoir isn't a perfect fit, but more of a hybrid, there's no need to panic. What I'm outlining is meant to be more of a general guideline—there are no hard and fast rules here. While some memoirs will certainly blur the lines between categories, every memoir can have its essence boiled down to a sentence or two, and that's really what I'm talking about when I say "hook." Here's a closer look at what kinds of memoirs you're going to find on the shelf at your local bookstore.

Travel Memoirs and Spiritual Quests

Travel memoirs take the reader along on a journey, whether it be to a picnic in the Italian countryside, a café in Greenwich Village in the 1950s, or to a spiritual retreat in India. While many memoirs focus on rich landscapes and everything the location has to offer—

culture, food, language, art, music, architecture, the people, etc.—
many memoirs today also feature a spiritual quest. This might be
found in the form of healing a broken heart, a search for romance,
or just an overall attempt to find new meaning in life. These memoirs are full of color and require a skilled writer, since descriptions
of the places visited—the landscapes, the towns, the buildings, the
sunsets, the food—may actually serve as characters in the memoir.
While *Under the Tuscan Sun* by Frances Mayes, *Eat, Pray, Love* by
Elizabeth Gilbert, and *An Italian Affair* by Laura Fraser are wonderful examples of travel memoirs, writers who want to feature a
strong sense of place or a quest in their work are by no means limited to traveling. *The Big House: A Century in the Life of an American Summer Home* by George Howe Colt tells the story of forty-two
summer family vacations under the roof of a sprawling house on
Cape Cod, while Linda Greenlaw's *The Hungry Ocean: A Swordboat Captain's Journey* takes the reader on a thirty-day fishing trip
in the Atlantic Ocean.

Food and Wine: Memoirs That Touch the Senses

I enjoy reading about food almost as much as I enjoy actually eating it, so I'm always glad that there is no shortage of food memoirs.
There is also a surprising amount of variety to be found in what one
might suspect to be a fairly blasé and straightforward category. You
can cozy up with a book full of wonderful recipes for shortbread
and jam embedded alongside tales of domestic bliss, or you can
decide you want to know what really goes on behind the swinging
doors in your typical restaurant kitchen (here's a tip, skip the hol-
landaise sauce). Food memoirs have become increasingly popular as
this category continually offers up fresh new material to a very devoted readership. Not only do we have marvelously written stories
about how chefs came to be passionate about food, but other writers
have pushed the envelope and shown us the underbelly of the restaurant industry. Famed food critic Ruth Reichl's trilogy of mem-

oirs *Tender at the Bone*, *Comfort Me With Apples* and *Garlic and Sapphires* are classic examples of a woman's love affair with food. Anthony Bourdain, while equally enamored with food, chose to express his love in a different fashion in his mega-bestseller *Kitchen Confidential: Adventures in the Culinary Underbelly*. He freely tosses around the f-word, talks about heavy drinking, sex in inappropriate places, childish pranks, and the horrors of spoiled mussels. Bourdain's candid take on the restaurant world shows that there is plenty of room for different voices in this genre. Laurie Colwin's beloved *Home Cooking: A Writer in the Kitchen* and *More Home Cooking: A Writer Returns to the Kitchen* are examples of memoirs you will refer to again and again. And Patricia Volk's *Stuffed: Adventures of a Restaurant Family* shows a slightly more wholesome, but equally character-driven, side of restaurant life to the one Anthony Bourdain shows us in his memoir.

I'll Take You There Memoirs

Have you ever wondered how well you would fare as a stripper? Is swinging around on that pole as easy as it looks? Could you follow the Old Testament word for word for a week much less an entire year? And if you did, would you be a better person because of it? "I'll Take You There" memoirs are often funny, always entertaining, and take the reader to a place they wouldn't normally dare go on their own. They sometimes have a "year in the life" quality, but by no means limit the writer to any particular time frame. They invite the reader into a new world, providing an inside look at places the average person would never normally have an opportunity to go. Diablo Cody's *Candy Girl: A Year in the Life of an Unlikely Stripper* showed that the inner workings of strip clubs (the strippers included) are more complex than anyone could have ever imagined. A.J. Jacob's *The Year of Living Biblically: One Man's Humble Quest to Follow the Bible as Literally as Possible* was full of surprises (eating crickets) and made some very unexpected stops along the way, including Appalachia and Amish country.

I Will Survive Memoirs

Some of the most successful memoirs in recent years fall into a category that could be described as the "I Will Survive" category. These memoirs deliver a message and capture the reader with powerful stories of self-discovery, soul-searching, healing, survival, and courage. Memoirs that fall into this section grab you by the heart and don't let go. While many of these memoirs are ultimately comforting—the journey is often defined by someone else's pain. Many such memoirs feature stories of abuse, addiction, death, and illness, but they also bring something else to the table that shows the reader that there is a light at the end of the tunnel. Jeannette Wall's astonishing climb from a childhood defined by deprivation to a stable life on New York City's Park Avenue is depicted with grace and candor in *The Glass Castle*. Kelly Corrigan's *The Middle Place* manages to tell the story of her cancer, as well as her father's terminal illness with charm and humor—showing us that being part of a big, boisterous family does actually make some of life's bigger challenges a little bit easier to manage. And while I didn't actually think I would make it through the first chapter of Kate Braestrup's *Here If You Need Me* (so heartbreaking was her story of becoming an accidental minister after her husband was struck and killed by a car while on duty as a state trooper in Maine), ultimately, I was able to make it past her raw writings on grief, as her take on family and spirituality proved incredibly comforting and her story came through, miraculously, without any clichés. Stories in this category can be tough to pull off (see comment about clichés), and obviously require having encountered a particularly tough set of circumstances. As is the case in all memoirs, strong writing is essential, even if in this category it may be tempting to lean on the reader's sympathy—doing so may result in a tedious read rather than one that people ultimately find inspiring.

Love and Relationship Memoirs

Love and relationships have always provided rich material for memoirs, and while you will certainly find your standard memoirs about romance among the titles here, I promise this category will exceed your expectations. One of the most moving relationship stories I have read in recent years was not one of love gone wrong, but of the ups and downs of female friendship. In her memoir, *Truth & Beauty*, Ann Patchett follows her friendship with writer and cancer survivor Lucy Grealy (herself the author of the highly regarded memoir *Autobiography of a Face*) as they struggle with Grealy's fame, drug addiction, and suicidal tendencies. This is a story about devotion as much as it is a memorial to Grealy, who died in 2002. Susan Richards' *Chosen by a Horse* is the charming and inspiring love story of both a broken woman and a broken horse. When Richards met "Lay Me Down," the horse was a mess—abused, sick, and malnourished. Against her better judgment, Richards found herself falling in love and learning more than she could have imagined about love, life, and relationships from this most unlikely of teachers. There is nothing wrong with an old-fashioned, textbook style romance, just know that there are many kinds of relationships to write about, and many different love stories worthy of telling.

Memoirs of Exploration

Memoirs that focus on explorations tend to have an investigational element. The author might be following a family secret—investigating a part of her life that, until recently, she never knew existed, as Bliss Broyard does in her memoir about her father's secret African-American roots in *One Drop*. As a practicing psychiatrist and leading authority in the field of bipolar disorder, Kay Redfield Jamison is in a very unique position to explore her mental illness, and write about it from a perspective of courage and understanding in her memoir *An Unquiet Mind*. Stephen King's wonderfully insightful *On Writing* is not only a helpful primer about the basics of writing, but an interesting look at the journey from ordinary, struggling writer to famous writer (who nevertheless still finds himself grappling with some of the very same issues). Memoirs that fall into this category cover a wide range of subjects, but also tend to have a narrative thread. This means that in addition to writing about the self, there is often another topic that the author is covering as well, which can be anything from race and identity, the craft of writing, or as we've seen with Jamison, mental health.

MEMOIRISTS SHARE THEIR FAVORITE MEMOIRS

SUZAN COLON, AUTHOR OF *CHERRIES IN WINTER*
I love Caroline Knapp's *Drinking: A Love Story* for her silken articulation of rough, murky emotions; Mary Cantwell's vivid word-paintings of the past in *Manhattan, When I Was Young*; and Anne Lamott's ability to be funny about potentially unfunny subjects in *Traveling Mercies: Some Thoughts on Faith.*

Break Your Story Into Key Memory Pieces

Now that we've had a chance to review the different categories of hooks and discuss the basic differences between hooks and themes, we can start digging into your memoir and see what hook-worthy gems just might be lying in wake. But figuring out how to find these gems can be challenging and the process and can feel a bit like backpedaling. After countless conversations, cups of coffee, and extended e-mail exchanges with authors, I've found that more often than not, the hook was there all along, the author just didn't know it. Hooks are often buried in too many details—extra stories and anecdotes, or reluctance to cut out a story because it involves a beloved friend or family member. It has been my experience that authors have their "ah-ha" moments about their memoirs while they are breaking down their stories, clearing out the clutter, and closely examining the pieces that are left to work with. This process can be done at any stage in the game, whether you have already completed a section of your memoir and are concerned that your memoir doesn't differentiate itself enough from what else is already out there, or if you are working with various sections, jotted down memories, journal pieces, character sketches, time lines of events, etc. The idea is to get all of the pieces of your work in one place and take a very close and critical look at what you have. One of most daunting parts of the memoir writing process is stepping back from your story and looking at it from a different perspective—the perspective of someone who *has not had the same experiences as you.* You need to "break the story down" and decide which pieces are crucial and which you can do without. Prepare to either mark your manuscript accordingly or catalog the pieces you have as items that will stay or go. Some questions to ask yourself are:

- Will this section be interesting to others?
- Is this character necessary to the larger story? Am I only keeping this person in my memoir for sentimental reasons? Do they really need to be here?
- Does this piece fit within the larger story I'm trying to tell?
- Is this section too long? Am I rambling?
- Is the amount of detail I have distracting from the greater story?

Put pieces that simply do not fit into your memoir in your ideas file. If you're concerned that certain sections are rambling, but can still be used in the memoir, mark them, and plan to edit them later. Don't let yourself get distracted by editing right now. The idea is to go through every single section and decide what stays and what goes. By taking the time to pare back your story and limit it to the most vibrant and essential details, a pattern will emerge that is often the beginning of the ever-coveted hook! What direction are these pieces taking you? Are they leading you to the original place you thought you were going or somewhere slightly different? Were you surprised to discover that while your ex-boyfriend didn't play a role in your memoir about going to culinary school your grandmother actually did? Did you stumble upon stories that ultimately mattered much more than you initially thought? Were you surprised by your beautiful descriptions of rural Mexico or your mouth-watering description of chocolate fondue? These remaining sections are your *key memory pieces* and provide important insight when it comes to narrowing down your hook. Key memory pieces are those surprising little sections that cause you to pause and actually reflect on a memory for a moment or two. Have you ever wondered why it sometimes takes an entire afternoon to clean out a closet or just a drawer? What initially sounds like a simple task inevitably turns into a long, winding road trip down memory lane. That's exactly the kind of journey we're talking about here. Those unexpected emotional jolts often hold hidden keys to parts of your story that need to be highlighted.

QUICK TIP: *I highly recommend starting an "ideas file" since, as most writers know, something you toss today often saves your ass tomorrow. So don't be afraid to put an idea aside for later. You have to make a vow right now to be honest with yourself. Be ruthless at this stage in the game and toss stuff that doesn't work for this project! Even if it just so happens that you had one of the most fascinating birthday parties in the history of ten-year-old birthday parties, it's not helping your cause if your memoir is about the Peace Corps. Put this in your ideas file and forget about it for now. Your memoir will thank you.*

Mining the Tiny Treasure Trove for Hook-Worthy Gems

You've eliminated the fluff, dutifully put all of the stories about your opera loving dog and senior prom into your ideas file and convinced yourself that your jerk ex-boyfriend has no place in a memoir about your move from the corporate world to culinary school. Well done! So what are you to do with these scraps of paper, journal entries, notes, and chapters? Now it's time to sit down, grab a notebook and pencil and take a closer look at what you have left. I recommend devoting one page of your notebook to each of the major themes that your memoir contains. Because these pages become so richly filled with bright ideas for hooks, I call them *tiny treasure troves*. Never underestimate the power of the smallest memory to become the biggest of ideas. For instance, if you're writing about leaving corporate America after a divorce to open a bakery with your sister, the pages of your notebook may include; FOOD, SURVIVAL, DIVORCE, and FAMILY. Now look carefully through your key memory pieces. Where do these pieces belong and what do they inspire? Catalog each key memory on the appropriate page and see where this leads. It is very likely that you will see a pattern developing—something that you may not have realized was there until now. Perhaps the FAMILY TREASURE TROVE has twenty items about sisterhood, including several hilarious stories that you hadn't realized were so colorful and fun to read. Once you have cataloged your key memory pieces, read through your treasure troves and consider the following:

- Does one of my key memory pieces inspire me to shift my focus?
- Does one of my key memory pieces feature a person who plays a key role in the story?
- Is there an unexpected emotional element that keeps making an appearance?

- Is one of the key memories a special setting or place that can provide a backdrop for a memoir?
- Have I personally experienced something unusual or unique that I can relay to others?
- Is one of the key memories adding an element to a common theme that no one has used before?

This boiled-down, cleaner version of your work can now be used as a fresh starting point, and you can prepare to start building your memoir up with the personal touches that a good hook gives a memoir in the following set of exercises.

Final Flourishes

You've determined the main ingredients necessary to tell your story and have a clearer idea of where your hook might take you. While you shouldn't let our hook take over the driving completely, you should let it guide you and help keep you on track. Now that you're more familiar with the most common types of memoirs, understand the difference between themes and hooks, have gathered your key memory pieces, and have been mining the tiny treasure troves, you should be able to see your material within a new context and feel ready to start working using your new foundation. Your hook is a building block—a spine from which to build and let your story flourish. Perhaps during the course of this chapter, you've discovered that your memoir is really more about friendship than romance, or maybe you now see that your strength as a writer is found in your descriptions of the places you've seen rather than your stories of the things you've done. Are your stories about cooking your grandmother's recipes the crown jewels in your collection? Have you decided that it's the year you spent in Africa that you want to focus on? Or are you planning to dust off the stories about how you left the mild Midwest for the wild world of New York City book publishing? Now that you discovered your core story, the one with the extraordinary, standout qualities that will make the reader select *your* book from all of the others on the shelf, you're ready to get to work!

> **QUICK TIP:** *Once you've identified your hook, set up a marketing file and start to keep track of any blogs, magazines, journals, support groups, interest groups, clubs, or websites that pertain to your topic. Come publication time, this file will become invaluable to marketing your book. You can plan to target all of these places prior to your memoir's publication, and provide any information about readings, author appearances, book group discussions, interviews, etc. Remember, publishers love a marketing savvy author! More on marketing in chapter eleven.*

 EXERCISE #1
WRITE YOUR OWN FLAP COPY

Good flap copy and catalog copy is so essential to a book's success that publishers often begin working on it before a manuscript is even completed. Flap copy and catalog copy are incredibly important marketing tools and must provide the sales team with exciting and memorable descriptions of a book that also manage to be clear and concise. So, as you might imagine, a good hook is crucial when pitching new titles to a book buyer. With this in mind, carefully read the flap copy of three of your favorite memoirs. How does the description hold up with your perception of what the memoir is about? Do you now look at your favorite memoir from a different perspective? Take a stab at writing the flap copy for your memoir. Since flap copy must give potential readers a sense of the story, its tone, and the overall direction of the book in a very limited amount of space, the publisher generally relies on the hook to capture the essence of the story. What did you discover when you boiled your story down to a few paragraphs? How does your flap copy compare to that of some of your favorite memoirs? Does this sound like a book you'd like to read?

 EXERCISE #2

PUSH YOUR THEME TO THE LIMIT

While the theme or topic for any given book may be fairly general, your hook will add that extra something special that truly makes the work *your* memoir. To find these extra elements, you may need to push yourself to the limit. Start by listing ten things that are unique about your situation. Nothing is too crazy—so don't be afraid if what you're writing down initially seems like it might be off topic. What makes your divorce different from your neighbor's? What makes your bout with cancer different from everyone else's? Keep in mind that the answers don't always have to be literal or terribly deep. Your husband told you he was leaving you via Facebook? Yes, that is definitely something to note. You didn't have to have a life-altering epiphany while undergoing chemotherapy, but if you bonded with the sweet child in the next room and that gave you the strength to go on, yes! Please tell us more about that! What else is on your list? What range of emotions does your list hit? Is it funnier or sadder than you anticipated? Is there something there that would make an especially good hook?

 EXERCISE #3

SHIFT YOUR FOCUS

Sometimes you can highlight your hook by simply shifting your focus onto a different part of your story. Elizabeth Gilbert's *Eat, Pray, Love* would have taken on a completely different feeling if the book had started off on her wedding day and had included the ups and downs of her marriage, and Joan Didion's *The Year of Magical Thinking* might have lacked it's initial dramatic punch had it not opened on the night of her husband's death but instead began earlier in their relationship. Select five different starting points for your memoir. Make a list of the key plot points from the five new starting positions. How does this change the scope of your story? Which key components change? What track does the memoir follow when starting from different positions? How does each new story feel? Where does each story end if you start from a different position?

 EXERCISE #4

WHAT KEEPS YOU UP AT NIGHT?

Finding your hook often takes time, persistence, and patience—and sometimes you have to listen to the little voice in your head that just won't shut up. I can't tell you how many book ideas have been born from my simply asking a desperate author, "So, what keeps you up at night?" If something is keeping you up, or even distracting you during the day, it's obviously important and worth exploring. Keep a notebook with you and start to note any ideas, no matter how crazy or obscure, any time these pesky thoughts cross your mind. If you find yourself daydreaming about "chocolate" or "champagne," maybe these words will steer you in the right direction. Ditto travel. If you're dreaming about "maps," maybe this is an interesting tangent to explore? Don't be afraid to break your subject down further. You never know what other interesting subtopics you might find, and the perfect hook could be right around the corner.

> **REALITY CHECK:** *Are you relying on your hook for too much? Remember, while a hook is essential for marketing your book properly, it is possible to lean on your hook too much. Even if you have a truly fantastic, one-of-a-kind story, substance must follow the hook. Are you following through with quality writing and a well thought-out story? A good hook is completely useless without these essential elements!*

RECOMMENDED READING

MEMOIRS WITH GOOD HOOKS
Edith's Story by Edith Velmans
An Unquiet Mind by Kay Redfield Jamison
Girl, Interrupted by Susanna Kaysen
The Tenth Muse by Judith Jones
The Last Lecture by Randy Pausch
The Big House by George Howe Colt
Another Life by Michael Korda
One Drop by Bliss Broyard

CHAPTER THREE:

Setting Your Parameters

 finished getting dinner, I set the table in the living room where, when we were home alone, we could eat within sight of the fire. I find myself stressing the fire because fires were important to us. I grew up in California, John and I lived there together for twenty-four years, in California we heated our houses by building fires. We built fires even on summer evenings, because the fog came in. Fires said we were home, we had drawn the circle, we were safe through the night. I lit the candles. John asked for a second drink before sitting down. I gave it to him. We sat down. My attention was on mixing the salad. John was talking, then he wasn't.

—from *The Year of Magical Thinking* by JOAN DIDION

Joan Didion's award-winning memoir *The Year of Magical Thinking* begins, not ends, with death. It is the sudden loss of her husband that launches her into the "year of magical thinking." This unexpected event provided a clear beginning to what was the most lauded and arguably most moving memoir of the year. The story started the second her husband's life ended—at that very moment the first "parameter" of the story was (very tragically) set. When attempting to translate a significant portion of your life's story, it is crucial, when dealing with a vast amount of material—an *entire lifetime* of memories—that you set limits early on and decide which portion of your life will prove to be the most colorful, provocative, and representative of the story you wish to tell. If limits aren't set early in the writing process, a story can easily get out of control, meander, and become completely disorganized. As you now know from chapter one, you are writing a memoir, not an autobiography! A well-crafted memoir will encapsulate a specific story that fits somewhere within the larger framework of your life. This chapter is about building that framework, or setting the parameters, of your story.

Thankfully, not all memoirs are written under such dark circumstances (although if you are an avid reader of memoirs, you know by now that a good number of them are), and the sudden and dramatic death of Didion's husband provided an obvious beginning to her story. But do all memoirs have such clear starting and, for that matter, ending points? Unless your story started when you received an unpleasant diagnosis, the day your spouse left, or—on the brighter side of things—when you won several hundred million dollars in the lottery, memoirs often start with more of a whimper than a bang. Ditto endings. Some memoirs end with complete resolution, some leave us at a comfortable middle point, while others leave us hanging a bit. How do you know when to end a story that may very well be still going on?

Setting your parameters isn't about blowing your reader away with a gripping first page (we'll get to that later), or wrapping up a complicated memoir with a perfectly poetic ending, but about sorting out your story before you find yourself buried in so many details—memories, ideas, facts, tangents, anecdotes—that you can't dig yourself back out. Without having a clear framework in mind before you start to tell your story, you are at risk of losing sight of the entire reason you started to write your memoir in the first place.

DON'T GO SEARCHING
FOR SOMETHING THAT ISN'T THERE

You're writing about your bucolic upbringing in a small town in Iowa where everyone loved each other and you went on to college even though you were dirt poor and didn't have shoes until you were fifteen, and then after winning a football scholarship, you became the town doctor beloved by all who married his high school sweetheart and eventually had four kids who were even more wonderful and noble than you. Should you start digging through your family files to see if you had any aunts who might have lived in the attic for a spell? Or ask around to see if you're related to any devil worshippers or ax murders? Do you need to get arrested in order to make your memoir marketable? No and NO. The parameters you set for your story can be very personal and subtle, or they may be big and unmistakable. This isn't about drama; you just need to keep your focus and work within the boundaries you've chosen. If you've decided that four years in the life of a small town doctor will make a great memoir, there is nothing wrong with opening your story with a scene from your waiting room. It doesn't need to be the scene of a grizzly accident. It's about making the decision to start you story at a certain point and stick with it. The key here is finding a starting point and setting that first parameter in a way that fits the tone, voice, and style of the memoir you are writing. Keep the following points in mind as you think about why some memoirist may have chosen to start and end their memoirs where they did.

The Good Parameter Checklist

- Good parameters will help to keep your memoir focused and organized.
- Good parameters will add to the story by creating an appropriate anchor from which your story will begin and end.
- Good parameters will fit in with the story you are telling.
- Good parameters will provide a provocative or engaging beginning and a satisfying ending point.
- Good parameters will help you determine which stories to use in your memoir and which should be put aside for another time.

Parameter Pitfalls

- The dreaded "I was born"—we've been over this, but it's worth bringing up again.
- Starting or ending with a story that isn't immediately relatable to the rest of the book.
- Starting with a character who won't be seen again until much later in the book.
- Starting or ending with a story because of its sentimental value—not because of its value to the memoir as a whole.

QUICK TIP: *When we talk about setting parameters, and figuring out "when" you're story begins, please note that I'm not talking in a hit-the-ground-running, first page of your book kind of way. Just remember this is a means of controlling the vast amount of material you've accumulated over a lifetime! If it works out as a literal beginning, great—if not, that's completely fine!*

FINDING YOUR MOMENT OF DISCOVERY

You understand the genre you're working in, you've pulled out your key memory pieces, and you've determined what your memoir's hook is going to be. Now you need to be sure you can place all of this material within a reasonable structure. How does a writer decide where to begin when a life story is so full of laughter, conversations, friendships, adventures, tragedies, and just day-to-day memories? Knowing how to *literally begin* telling a story is a huge challenge for any writer—whether your story begins the day you leapt out of an airplane, or whether your story starts more subtly, such as when you began to realize that your marriage was over. Do you start with a description of what you were thinking? Or maybe you start with the conversation you had with your husband when you woke up that day? Maybe your story started while you were watching the clock while waiting for your husband to come home on your anniversary—or maybe it was the day he stopped asking you if you wanted a second cup of coffee. Regardless of the amount of drama surrounding your personal story, it's important that as a memoirist—a person recording your own personal history—that you manage to take a step back and recognize when it was that your own personal journey began. This is your *moment of discovery*, and it sets the first parameter of your memoir. I realize this sounds a bit grand, but I promise it's not as dramatic as it seems, and thinking along these lines when planning your memoir will prove to be incredibly helpful.

"Your dog is in the elevator."

These six simple words changed writer Abigail Thomas's life forever. After her doorman told her "your dog is in the elevator," she quickly learned that her husband, who was out walking the dog, had been hit by a car and had sustained a traumatic brain injury. Her memoir *A Three Dog Life*, is a moving and eloquent account of her life with a man who lives in the continual present. While I'm sure the author wishes she had never heard those words, it is her skill as a memoirist that enables her to recognize them as a "moment of discovery." It was that sentence that signaled the beginning of her new life, as difficult as it may be. The moment of discovery is the key moment signaling that the memoirist's story has begun. Thomas recalls the moment she heard those words very accurately:

> Monday, April 24, at nine forty at night, our doorman Pedro called me on the intercom. "Your dog is in the elevator," he said. The world had just changed forever, and I think I knew it even then.

I think what makes Thomas's moment of discovery so astonishing is that it is such an incredible mixture of ordinary and bizarre.

The situation immediately suggested to her, without presenting the information of the accident itself, that something was desperately wrong. Several connections must have been made in her mind at once for her to realize that this simple scenario—of her dog, returning home from his walk out on the city streets alone—was unfortunately, just the beginning of a tragic and dramatic story. She was able to pinpoint the beginning of all of the massive changes she was about to experience back to this one particular moment. Not only does this moment of discovery provide the first parameter of her story, which will keep her story working within a framework, but it is also engaging, powerful, and meaningful and draws the reader in right from the beginning.

LAUNCHING YOUR STORY

The Two Kinds of Beginnings

We all have our moments of discovery, regardless of the kind of memoir we're writing. It doesn't matter if it's happy in tone, or tragic like Frank McCourt's. There is a moment we can look back to and realize, "Yeah, this is pretty much when all of this started." But depending on the nature of our stories, our moments of discovery may have occurred under very different circumstances. Thomas's is very clear cut. Her husband was in an accident. She can look at a calendar and note the exact date and time that her life changed. For many of us, the beginnings of our stories are more nebulous. Elizabeth Gilbert's story could have started on a number of occasions: when she realized she didn't want a baby, when her divorce was final, when she got on that plane to Italy, etc. It was more of a choice for her—*it's personal*. Her story developed over time, so as a memoirist, she needed to comb through her memories to determine what would be a meaningful first parameter for her.

Cornerstone Days

The day a loved one is gravely injured is life changing, and for obvious reasons, it makes complete sense for a memoir to start from this place in a person's story. Cornerstone days certainly don't always have to be tragic, but they present clear and undeniable evidence that a person's life story has been permanently altered. Let's take a look at some other memoirs that begin with cornerstone days.

THE MIDDLE PLACE BY KELLY CORRIGAN

A thirty-six-year-old woman who is happily married and the mother of two, and who still very much considers herself to be daddy's little girl, finds herself diagnosed with an aggressive form of breast cancer. Her story, as a woman dealing with her illness, while also contending with her roles as a mother, wife, and daughter, "sees" herself as a cancer patient for the first time while simply getting situated in the waiting room and filling out a pile of forms. It is while doing these perfunctory tasks that she realizes she is seriously ill:

> From a distance, I watch myself gingerly approach cancer. It is outside me. It is abstract. I fill out the forms, and everything seems so loaded . . .

HURRY DOWN SUNSHINE BY MICHAEL GREENBERG

Hurry Down Sunshine follows the summer when Greenberg's daughter Sally, who was only fifteen at the time, has a complete mental breakdown and is hospitalized. It is a very emotional and chilling memoir of mental illness, made more so because of the age of the victim. Greenberg comes home to find that his daughter had been behaving erratically while spending time with a friend—running into oncoming traffic believing she could stop cars, grabbing passersby, and yelling at the police. Surprised and confused by her behavior, he soon finds that this is just the beginning. Sally begins ranting that "genius is childhood" and that she must get to the "Sunshine Café" which is really just a rundown lunch counter

---

> sandwiched between a pornographic bookstore and an AIDS hospice. Greenberg is horrified to learn that this isn't Sally's first visit, and they consider her to be a nuisance. She is sworn at by the proprietor and asked to leave. She is given dirty looks by otherwise friendly neighbors who now seem afraid of her. Overwhelmed and frightened for his daughter's safety, she is taken to the emergency room and put into psychiatric care.
>
> *I absorb the shock of seeing her through his cold glare: a pariah. My heart sinks. Our neighbor Lou, this summary eviction from the Sunshine Café. . . I remember a legend of Solomon: outwitted by a demon, he is thrown out of Jerusalem and the demon takes over as king.*

Does your memoir begin with a cornerstone day? Is there a certain undeniable life-changing event that your story is based around? Then yes, your story definitely follows the cornerstone day format. So while you know what the first parameter of your memoir is, how will you use a moment of discovery to share your story with readers in a manner that accurately reflects the true nature of your experience? How will you guide your readers through what you felt? When thinking about relaying that moment of discovery, that moment when you knew that your life was, at that very second, completely different, think about the following.

- What was the most surprising thing that went through my mind while my situation was happening? What was the strangest reaction I had?
- When I remember that day, what do I think about the most?
- If there is something I could make people understand about what happened, what would it be?

While Elizabeth Gilbert's odyssey in *Eat, Pray, Love* may never have taken place had she not found herself, after months of unhappiness, doing something as ordinary as laying on the bathroom floor praying to a god she wasn't sure she even believed in, it's important to note that at that moment, what she was doing was extraordinary *to her*. Those are the moments you want to think about when reflecting back on your cornerstone day. It is Gilbert's ability to understand that the place she has come to (in this case praying on the bathroom floor) means that there is absolutely no other choice at this point than to leave her marriage. It's a simple image, but it packs a punch nevertheless, and it gets the reader hooked into whatever it is that she's going to do next.

> **REALITY CHECK:** *I don't mean to sound flip, but if it is your intention to become a published memoirist, and you are writing a memoir that begins with a "cornerstone day" just remember, a sad story doesn't make up for bad writing. As an agent, I receive literally hundreds of proposals for memoirs for all manner of tragic situations, and while I'm truly sorry that each and every person has that material, it's not your story alone that's going to get you published. Regardless of your situation, you'll have to work hard to get your manuscript in A+ shape.*

MEMOIRISTS SHARE THEIR FAVORITE MEMOIRS

KELLY CORRIGAN, AUTHOR OF *THE MIDDLE PLACE* AND *LIFT*
It's a total toss-up between *Remembering Denny* by Calvin Trillin (I'm also a huge fan of *About Alice*) and *An Exact Replica of a Figment of My Imagination* by Elizabeth McCracken. McCracken's writing is a real model for me. The topics she writes about could be maudlin and over dramatic, verging on melodrama, but somehow she does it without manipulating the reader into some kind of emotional reaction.

REFLECTIVE BEGINNINGS

And what about those of us with interesting stories that begin with a subtle, more Oprah-esque "ah-ha" moment? What about memoirs that tell stories that are developed over time rather than starting with the sturm and drang you get with a cornerstone day? Do these memoirs still have a moment of discovery? And if they do, how do you find them? The answer is yes, they still do— it's just a slightly different way of thinking about the material. Even though memoirs that are more reflective in nature may not have the initial drama of a memoir, such as *The Year of Magical Thinking* (and that's not really such a bad thing is it?), all memoirs are ultimately about examining the little details in life that make it worth examining. Whatever story you're telling, it can likely be traced back to a few specific moments, memories, or ideas.

In his memoir about his life as a bookseller, *The Yellow Lighted Bookshop*, Lewis Buzbee recounts his life as both a lover of books and a bookseller. He thinks back on his "need to read" and realizes "it's tied to the *Weekly Reader* and Miss Baab's fourth-grade classroom and the lazy wonder of those afternoons." While this statement is certainly free of the drama we've come to expect from memoirs, it nevertheless elicits an emotional response. When I read that passage, I immediately remembered the excitement of selecting new books from the Scholastic Book Club, and the anticipation that surrounded their arrival. There was nothing more thrilling than to come back from lunch and find a book in the Little House series by Laura Ingalls Wilder or a mini Shaun Cassidy bio (give me a break, it was the 1970s) sitting on my desk. And I would have to agree with Buzbee that the book club definitely played a role in shaping me as a reader. This memory of his clicked with me and got me wrapped up in his story even though it doesn't have the same breathtaking punch-in-the-gut jumping off point that Greenberg's does. A reflective beginning can therefore be as effective as a more dramatic one. Let's look at a few other examples of memoirs that have reflective beginnings.

MANHATTAN, WHEN I WAS YOUNG
BY MARY CANTWELL

Mary Cantwell's *Manhattan, When I Was Young* is another example of a memoir that uses a reflective beginning. The reason for her move to New York City seems simple on the surface—she's a new college graduate looking to make her way in the world. But as her story progresses, her father's influence proves to hold more weight than she initially realized:

> No, what pulled me to New York, apart from the young man I was to marry, was my father's promise. 'Don't you change, don't you dare change,' he would say when I came home from school in tears because I hadn't been elected to this or that or because somebody had called me a showoff for writing so many book reports. 'Someday you'll live in a place where there are lots of people like you.' My guess is he meant academe, a world that he revered and that he believed welcomed the chatty, the gaffe-prone, the people with more brains than sense. But I bored with tests, bored with papers, and cursed with a mayfly's attention span, thought of something speedier. I thought of a world in which you 'raced' to the subway, 'hopped' the shuttle, 'grabbed' a cab. Infatuated with its pace, I thought of New York.

Cantwell arguably spends just as much time in New York chasing her father's ghost as she does chasing her dreams, which naturally adds an interesting layer to her story.

KITCHEN CONFIDENTIAL BY ANTHONY BOURDAIN

After describing several meals in France where his parents had to deal with Bourdain's and his young brother's insistence on ordering hamburgers and Cokes, his parents finally gave up and left them in the car while they enjoyed a meal at the famed La Pyramide restaurant. He and his brother were left in the car for three hours . . .

> I remember it well, because it was such a slap in the face. It was a wake-up call that food could be important, a challenge to my natural belligerence. By being denied, a door opened.

Bourdain goes on to say:

> *I had plenty of time to wonder: What could be so great inside those walls? They were eating in there. I knew that. And it was certainly a Big Deal; even at a witless age nine, I could recognize the nervous anticipation, the excitement, the near-reverence with which my beleaguered parents had approached this hour.*

But what's really interesting to me is what he says next:

> *Things changed. I changed after that.*

Apparently, the mere idea that he could be missing out on something—anything better than steak haché was enough to send a nine-year-old Anthony Bourdain on a mission. He reports that from that point on, there was nothing France had to offer from a culinary perspective that he couldn't handle. He goes on to list sweetbreads, kidneys, small whole fish, stinky cheese, red wine (contraband), tripe, and, perhaps most fondly, oysters, as some of his favorite foods from that fateful trip. Bourdain's excitement over his first oyster could not be more vivid; it's obvious this was a life-changing trip. It's a fantastic passage—watching a kid grow from total brat and self-proclaimed "Ugly American" to mini-foodie, all because his parents played it strict and decided to leave the kids in the car.

QUICK TIP: *Your "moment of discovery" may give you a few clues as to who the audience of your book may be. If your moment of discovery occurred during a "cornerstone day," you might want to think about support groups, etc., that may be interested in your story. If your book starts with a "reflective beginning," start thinking about interest groups, websites, blogs, etc., that share common interests and might be interested in buying your book. More on this in chapter twelve.*

The Second Parameter: Working With the End in Site

Perhaps one of the biggest challenges of memoir writing is knowing when to end your own story. How do you know when to end a story that is obviously still going on? While it may seem counter intuitive to know how to end a book before you've truly gotten into the thick of things, I'm a firm believer that, when writing a memoir, it is best to work with the end in site. One of the biggest advantages to memoir writing is that you usually have access to most of the materials right up front—since the story is largely comprised of your own memories. Since memoirists have the advantage of knowing what they have to work with, you can actually start to envision where you would like your story to go and start to plan how you would like to go about getting the reader to that ending point.

As with memoirs that start off with cornerstone days, some memoirs are going to have natural endings, such as when a battle with a long illness ends, when a person leaves a difficult situation, after a particular decision is made, or even after a trip has ended. But when a situation is ongoing, how do you possibly decide when it is appropriate to end your own story other than just running out of steam and typing THE END? I think it's important to remember that the ending of a memoir means the ending of *your story.* With memoir writing, it is the author's job to place the second parameter appropriately in the story to give the reader closure. While the memoirists story may change the very next day, or maybe the following week, or not for several years, at some point a decision needs to be made about how much of the story it is appropriate to relay in this book. Let's take a look at how some memoirists chose to close their stories. Remember, I'm not necessarily giving anything away here. The authors have selected a few moments that they feel are a good representation of what was happening in their lives at the time their story was winding down.

HURRY DOWN SUNSHINE BY MICHAEL GREENBERG

I think this is a particularly interesting example, because as you probably remember, this memoir started off in a rather dramatic

---

fashion with a cornerstone day that featured the author's teenage daughter literally losing her mind. I was completely moved by the second parameter of this story. Take a look at this passage describing a period where he and his daughter are able to have a completely normal conversation:

> Then, one evening in late August, everything changes. Sally and I are standing in the kitchen. I have spent the day at home with her, working on my script for Jean-Paul. "Would you like a cup of tea?" I ask. "That would be nice. Yes. Thank you." "With milk?" "Please. And honey." "Two spoonfuls?"

The logistics about the cup of tea continue just a tad longer; I think you're probably already starting to get my point. But just in case, Greenberg goes on to say:

> It's as if a miracle has occurred. The miracle or normalcy, of ordinary existence. Following Sally's lead, I act as if nothing unusual has happened. And by all appearances, to her nothing unusual has happened; she seems unaware of the change. I think to myself: I'll remember this conversation—this seemingly insignificant exchange—as the moment when Sally returned.

Note that he says "returned." He didn't say she was "cured"—or anything to indicate that this ordeal was completely over. This is memoir; it's about life, and the bottom line is that life is just *not that neat*. If the author were waiting for the perfect cure for something as unpredictable and as complicated as mental illness to arrive before he finished his story, he likely would never have published it.

A THREE DOG LIFE BY ABIGAIL THOMAS

In *A Three Dog Life*, Abigail Thomas walks into her husband's room one day to find, quite unexpectedly, that he is remembering some details about his accident. After writing an entire memoir that deals with her very particular kind of loss, and carving out a new life for herself, she is confronted with a man who she realizes "wants to remember what she is trying to forget." They talk about the accident and how she reacted. It's one of the more lucid conversations she recounts in the book. But then Thomas asks her husband if he knows how long they've been married. His answer? "About a year." Just as quickly as she had her husband back, he slips away again. But then after reminding him that the real answer is more like seventeen, he smiles at his wife and adds this, "Our life has been so easy that the days glide by." Is there a more perfect place to end her story than with this brief moment showing the two different lives she has with her husband? The one who is lost—and can't function, and says the craziest things—but also with a hint of the man she married—the man she fell in love with and knows her, remembers their marriage, and can still say the most romantic things.

So if your memoir cannot be wrapped up easily at an obvious point in time, think about the following things when making a plan to tie things up. Be sure to refer to your key memory pieces for clues. You may hit upon something that can help you.

- Is there an ongoing theme in my memoir that I can come full circle to? Is there a memory or event that I can use to demonstrate this?
- Is there a specific age or year of my life I want to end with? (If so, be sure you know why—how does this play into your memoir as a whole?)
- Was there a decision I made or an action I took at some point in my story that changed the direction of my life?
- Was there an internal change that took place? An emotional response to something that happened that played a key role in my story?

 EXERCISE #1
YOUR DOG IS IN THE ELEVATOR

Abigail Thomas astutely realizes her entire life changed the second she found out that oddly, her "dog was in the elevator." Her ability to recognize this detail as representative of something larger and darker is what makes her such a skilled memoirist. It's my feeling that every writer whose memoir begins with a cornerstone day has a moment when they clearly know that his life is never going to be the same. For Kelly Corrigan, this moment may have come while filling out forms in the waiting room. For Michael Greenberg, he knew his daughter's situation was serious when he saw their neighbor looking at her with both fear and disgust—as you would a frightening homeless person. In all of these cases, the moment of discovery wasn't necessarily the moment the authors received a specific piece of news, but the moment they themselves pieced together the information in a way that was meaningful to them. Think about your situation—whether it be a divorce, a death, an illness, or another kind of loss. When did the situation become real to *you*? Remember, this is your memoir, so I'm not talking about reality necessarily. Obviously being told "you have breast cancer" makes the situation pretty real. But maybe it didn't become real to you until you realized you couldn't run the marathon next year. Or maybe your divorce didn't feel final when you signed the papers (again, yes, pretty real), but when you got out the Christmas tree and put it up by yourself for the first time. It's your moment of discovery, so be sure you're conveying it in a way that feels authentic to you.

EXERCISE #2

OPENING DOORS

Bourdain's quote "by being denied, a door opened" always stuck in my mind—even years after I read *Kitchen Confidential*. Disappointment, loss, and even tragedy are not uncommon themes in memoirs. However, it is also common for people writing memoirs to feature another, more positive and inspiring side to their stories. What doors opened up for you as a result of your disappointment or loss? Is there something you were denied that turned out to be a huge blessing? Make a list of what opened up for you. Would some of these points of entry make a good starting point for your memoir?

EXERCISE #3

WHAT MAKES YOU UNCOMFORTABLE?

If you're still feeling unsure about when your story really started, maybe there's a bit more inner searching you need to do. Remember, you're writing a memoir! Committing your life story to paper is sure to bring up

loads of memories, some easier to handle than others. And I'm not talking about the "oh hey, I think it's possible I was abducted by an alien and
spent my early adulthood living on Mars and that's why those formative
years are a blur!" kind of memories that would likely require some professional help. Writing a memoir, even one that's ultimately happy, can
begin with some painful reminders of a person you used to be. If you're
finding yourself with a big, gaping hole in your memoir, or you're finding
the beginning or your story painful to revisit, it might be time to think
about why this particular portion is difficult to handle. You might want to
consider dealing with this section in another format until you feel more
comfortable with the material. A personal essay, extensive journaling, a
blog entry, short story, or magazine article might allow you to explore
this portion of your story and get over any hurdles that are stopping you
from moving forward with the rest of your memoir.

PART TWO

the memorist's toolbox

You've dutifully been reading memoirs (and if you've stumbled upon any obscure ones, remember to e-mail me, I want to know about them!). You've been archiving old photographs, letters, and mementos—and probably wondering, are we going to start writing already? The answer is *yes*. I promise all of this preparation, and the planning to follow will be well worth your time, as it really can prevent some of those awful, "what is this massive disorganized mess I've written I have no choice but to totally start over" moments that make you just want to give up. Writing a book is a marathon, and as you've heard a million times before, slow and steady is the way to go. But since you're well acquainted with the genre, and after all that self-archiving, you're more than ready to start learning about the Memoirist's Toolbox. These tools will enable you to put together a clear and concise, well-organized, lively, and engaging memoir. This toolbox will not only give you the basics of structure, format, and voice, but also enable you to perform some fairly advanced maneuvers that a memoir writer needs to survive in what is arguably a pretty tough market right now. You'll learn about marketing hooks, moments of discovery, setting parameters for your memoir, and even the delicate art of "breaking rules correctly." These are the tools I've been using to help my clients get published for years, and they work. Let's get started.

CHAPTER FOUR:

TOOL #1:
Structure—Designing Your Memoir's Blueprint

S tructure, foundation, format. Take your pick. All three of these words can basically be used to describe the way an author chooses to build her story. I'll admit it, they all sound pretty boring, right? And an entire section of a book on structure? I know, if I were you I would be reaching for the remote control, too. *Law & Order* rerun anyone? However, I assure you, structure is quite possibly one of the most overlooked and under appreciated aspects of the memoir. There really is much room for play when it comes to structure, even though until recently, it was pretty much believed that messing around with structure was best left to novelists. Wrong! I'm here to tell you that memoirists can have a field day with structure. If you need to inject some life or energy into your memoir, structure is one of the best ways to do it. So what exactly is this "structure" I'm blathering on about?

DEFINING STRUCTURE

Structure generally refers to the overall plan for how you're going to relay the story you want to tell. When I talk to my authors about structure, we talk about not only what makes sense for their material, but what would be an interesting and unique way to showcase their story. What kind of foundation would best show off their strengths as a writer? What kind of structure would best complement what this particular book has to offer the reader? If you think about it, most books, memoirs especially, don't always smoothly move from point A to point B. More often than not, there's some moving back and forth in time, or perhaps the narrator interjects his own voice at some point. Maybe there are two different story lines that are being woven together.

How do you figure out what kind of structure is the best fit for you story? The good news is that there are no specific rules when it comes to structure. You're not going to find a book at the library that provides a neat and tidy detailed list of memoir structures to choose from. Why is this good news? Because it means you are free to play and make up something that is a perfect match for your particular work. There is no need to worry about fitting into a defined structure that already exists. Yes, I know that sounds kind of intimidating and scary, but as long as you can follow these guidelines, you can feel comfortable working within a "do it yourself" structure.

1. Your structure should provide a clear path for the reader to follow even if it weaves in and out of different time periods.
2. Your structure should offer something new and exciting rather than copy an already existing structure. Please note I'm not saying you need to reinvent the wheel, but please see my warning about trends further on in the chapter (see page 78).
3. Your structure should work to clarify the story rather than complicate it.
4. Your structure should serve as something more than a clever gimmick.

Keep in mind that your structure will also help you stay organized and focused and shouldn't overpower your material. It can be tempting to try to decide on a structure first, and then force your material into the foundation you've decided upon. But I caution you against trying to push your work into something that might not be the right fit. You risk ending up with a structure that feels gimmicky and awkward. The structure should support your prose; it shouldn't be running the show.

Let's look at some memoirs that have especially interesting structures. As you know from chapter one, memoirs tend to have a particular theme. Some of these themes may lend themselves well to certain kinds of structures, while other writers may have found an entirely unique way to present material that also falls into the same theme.

GIRLS OF TENDER AGE BY MARY-ANN TIRONE SMITH

I have never encountered a memoir that so gracefully ties together two such different stories. In her hilarious and equally horrifying memoir of growing up in Hartford, Connecticut, Smith tells a warm and charming story of growing up in an unusual household in what seems like picture-perfect 1950s America. While her family is full of unusual characters—her mother is nervous and seems to always be on the verge of a breakdown; and her brother is seriously autistic long before such things were properly diagnosed—her upbringing feels oddly typical of a post-World War II family, although perhaps more complicated and colorful. On the flip side, the author is puzzled as to why there is a big gaping hole in some of her childhood memories. Tirone-Smith comes up with a very effective way of investigating this lapse in memory, which also happens to be a brilliant way of tying her two narratives together.

Tirone-Smith starts out by giving the reader some information about her early years in the "D Section of the Charter Oak Terrace in Hartford, Connecticut" where her father describes their "socioeconomic level as Working Stiffs." We learn about their coal furnace, the "truly impoverished" kids who come to school with shaved heads because of lice, her incredibly nervous but possibly psychic mother, her autistic brother, her colorful cast of relatives, and her mother's tendency toward violence. The chapter ends, and suddenly we are presented with the biographical information of Robert Nelson Malm, a man born in the 1920s on the West Coast.

We have no idea why we are being given this information, but it's clear that he's not gotten off to a good start in life, and the author throws in one fact to give the reader an indication that he is an unsavory character. What's interesting about this treatment is that it catches your attention rather than throwing you off. She limits the section about Robert Nelson Malm to one brief page, but is sure to present the reader with one fact that is most certainly going to get you to sit up and pay attention. It signals to you that this character is going to play an important role in the story, and while you have no clue what the role is yet, it doesn't matter. You're hooked, and want to know more. Had she gone on for several more pages about his background, with us not knowing how he was going to fit into the story, we might have lost interest or become confused. Tirone-Smith continues in this fashion. Doling out more information about her own life—letting us luxuriate in her home, her family life, her challenges—while now and again presenting us with just a little bit more about the mysterious, although clearly dangerous, Robert Nelson Malm. She's building tension, building a narrative, and signaling to the reader that this is more than a story about a young girl growing up in Hartford, Connecticut. This is what structure is all about. Had the author not alternated the sections in this fashion, she would not have built tension and suspense like she did. What could have been a simple story about growing up on the post-World War II East Coast becomes a much larger story about the murder of a young girl and the effect it had on a quiet town like Hartford, Connecticut.

THE MIDDLE PLACE BY KELLY CORRIGAN

To open up Corrigan's memoir, you wouldn't think that this book had all that much going on in the structure department. The chapters are quite simply labeled as they are: "chapter 9" (which is a totally reasonable way to go about labeling your chapters by the way). She also notes the dates for each chapter, such as "Saturday, August 21st." Nothing particularly mind blowing about that right? But once you get into the flow of *The Middle Place*, you quickly see that there is a lovely rhythm to what's going on here, and there is, in fact, a simple and elegant structure that's quietly being erected. Her story follows a few different themes, and her memoir flows effortlessly from one topic to the other, ultimately creating a structure. *The Middle Place*, which as you may remember from chapter two, details Corrigan's battle with breast cancer. But that's not all. The memoir also covers a variety of issues, namely, what it's like to be "George Corrigan's daughter," a mother of two, and ultimately stuck in that place where you need to be taken care of while taking care of someone else. Moving from one area to the next, she lets her themes create a pattern that ultimately creates her structure for her. Very simple, but very effective. Working with a structure such as Corrigan's is, of course, about good writing—but it's also about knowing your material extraordinarily well, and knowing how you can showcase your story's strengths to make it more compelling and relatable.

HOW I LEARNED TO SNAP BY KIRK READ

Kirk Read's upbringing in the Shenandoah Valley screams all-American family. His mother was a homemaker and his father was career military. So what happens when the youngest child prefers listening to alternative music and writing in journals to dating cheerleaders and playing sports? *How I Learned to Snap* is a delightfully unexpected in that it is completely lacking any sense of blame or victimhood. While it is easy to get caught up in the fun tales of 1980s high school antics, you can't help but see that there was real suffering taking place, and to admire that this writer is neither bitter nor carrying any anger. One of the reasons this memoir, while painful at times, is so pleasant to read is that the author manages to tell entire stories within his short chapters. This enables him to introduce lots of characters and situations into the memoir—adding color, texture, and more fun with each new section. While Read plays a central unifying role in the book, he's able to bring other people to life, just long enough for us to get a good sampling. Kirk Read knows that storytelling is one of his strengths (and he spends quite a bit of time traveling the country doing live readings too—which are excellent and *always* sold out) and his structure is designed to reflect that. The following section is about Kirk's "emotional girlfriend Valerie."

Valerie was my emotional girlfriend. That's how she signed the notes she'd pass me in eleventh grade English, right under the nose of Ms. Coffey. Luckily, if Ms. Coffey really liked a student, they were beyond reproach. I can't count the hours I spent after school, confessing to Ms. Coffey my every conceivable intimacy. When I came out to her in a fourteen-page essay on Kate Chopin's The Awakening, she wrote a response in red ink that filled almost as many pages. She gave me an A and let me get away with murder for the rest of the year. God bless Ms. Coffey.

Valerie had come to us from Mississippi, where she'd apparently had a lot of religion in her life. She was Baptist and heavily involved with Young Life, a Christian organization that takes kids on camping trips for fireside indoctrination. Valerie actually lured me to one of their events, which was replete with earnest teenagers singing Michael W. Smith songs and professing their love for Jesus. During the campfire circle everyone started witnessing about Christ and testifying about how they'd found their faith. These children were like fifteen. When they got around to me, I said, "I'm not really into the God thing. I came because Valerie told me we'd play lots of games." Valerie turned as white as the turtleneck she wore almost daily, with a gold cross that dangled between her "not-there-yet breasts.

I left the circle shortly after several college students, in front of everyone, tried to save me with their dramatic tales of conversion. One young woman worked up tears as she recounted how she'd been brought to her knees by the Lord, whereupon I went back to my cabin. If God had to go to such lengths to invite people to his birthday party, I reasoned, He probably wasn't serving very good cake.

This section actually consists of a good portion of the entire chapter which ends in Valerie's surprising confession that she's a lesbian. In this short section, Read manages to tell an entire story, show how difficult and confusing it is to be a gay adolescent, and if you read the entire book you can see how these stories effort-lessly build on top of each other and read. This is a perfect ex-ample of how an author can use his strengths as a writer to guide the structure of his book.

MEMOIRISTS SHARE THEIR FAVORITE MEMOIRS

KIRK READ, AUTHOR OF *HOW I LEARNED TO SNAP*
My favorite memoir is *Monster: Living Off the Big Screen* by John Gregory Dunne. He levels with you about how sleazy it is to write for Hollywood. If you have a single glittery delusion about Holly-wood, Uncle John will disabuse you of that. As a rule, I love a cau-tionary book by someone much smarter than me, especially if he was married to Joan Didion.

A BRIEF HISTORY OF ANXIETY: YOURS AND MINE
BY PATRICIA PEARSON

Spontaneous liver failure. Eruption of the mega-volcano at the bot-tom of Yosemite. I mean, did you even know that existed? Spontane-ous explosion of the car she is riding in. These are just a few of the things that make novelist, essayist, and journalist Patricia Pearson anxious. She does note however, that some of the more common things that people are typically afraid of, such as house fires, breast cancer, and crime, don't phase her in the least. So what does this neurotic-sounding journalist and her fear of cows (yes, that's an-other one of them) have to do with structure? Basically, her laundry list of what she's afraid of is actually a great way—both funny and grabbing—to set the reader up for her exploration of anxiety. If you think back to that section on themes, Pearson's memoir falls into the exploration category. She's telling her own personal story, but also planning to explore anxiety on a larger level by using her jour-nalistic skills to consult experts and interview other anxiety suffer-ers. She moves on to use the bird flu as her first major jumping-off point. Reading a bulletin from the U.S. Department of Health and

Human Services that a pandemic is inevitable, her first reaction is to buy freeze-dried vegetables, order a tin of powered butter that is to be mixed with "27 cups of water," and to read "cooking with canned foods." She is able to use herself and her particular anxiety as a jumping-off point. She's anxious enough to start ordering survival materials from a company called Survival Acres. What better point in the memoir than to launch her investigation? She then begins to document how other panickers are reacting, such as a mother in Texas who washes her hands until they bleed and has already bought Christmas and birthday gifts for her kids so they can still celebrate while in quarantine. Wow. And since Pearson is a journalist as well as a memoirist, she knows that this is the perfect time to talk to an expert about what is known as "hypothetical analytical planning," otherwise known as *I need an Ambien refill.* The combination of Pearson's experience, the stories of other people suffering from acute anxiety as well as commentary from experts presents an incredibly funny yet informative exploration of anxiety. This is not a painful-to-read, one woman's story of her knees shaking in her boots and not being able to leave the house. Nor is it merely the story of a woman just laughing at how silly she can be (cows! Really!?!). *A Brief History of Anxiety* ultimately comes off as the story of someone who has recognized she has a problem that is both serious and at times debilitating and has decided to do something about it and is on this quest. It's also very clear the author hasn't lost her sense of humor, which makes the work all the more enjoyable to read.

> **REALITY CHECK:** *If you are interested in writing a memoir that does X, be honest with yourself about your credentials. What kind of experience do you bring to the table? If you aren't an experienced journalist, keep in mind that a publisher is going to expect you to be an expert in the particular field that you're interested in writing about. Before you start to panic about your credentials, see chapter eleven where we talk about building a platform.*

FINDING YOUR BEST FIT

Okay, I can imagine what you're thinking. It's probably something like, "So we've looked at the structure of just a few of the literally thousands of memoirs that are out there, and now I'm supposed to be able to magically figure out what structure is the best fit for my material?" Yeah, I realize that showing just a few examples can only help so much, but I hope those examples showed you that you can be really subtle with your structure, like Kelly Corrigan and Kirk Read, or you can be a little more dramatic with it like, Patricia Pearson or Mary-Ann Tirone Smith. Obviously, you have the freedom to do just about anything you want, but know that structure can be the star of the show, if you have a strong supporting cast of story and good writing. I know it sounds overwhelming, but you probably have a better idea about what kind of structure you'd like to follow than you realize. Don't worry, I'm not going to throw you to the wolves on this one. I'm going to walk you through a series of steps to help you see what kind of structure might be a good fit for your memoir. Ultimately, it's about what kind of framework you're most comfortable working in that also adds marketable value to your memoir. These steps should give you some hints about what kind of structure might actually already be lurking in the material you've already been working with. It's probably a good idea to make some notes as you read these next few pages. What you learn about your writing style may prove to be extraordinarily helpful.

STEP #1:
What Does Your Writing Style Say About You?

You can either look at pages of a manuscript you've already been working on, or you can look through journals, or simply think about writing exercises you've done in the past. What kind of exercises are you most drawn to? Are you the kind of writer who likes to wrap things up as tightly as possible within each chapter? Can all of your pieces stand on their own as individual stories or fit together into a larger work? Or are you the kind of writer who likes to use hints or perhaps even a bit of suspense to engage the reader and urge them to continue reading on? Do you prefer writing longer pieces? If so, how do you envision longer sections coming together?

Here are my notes on my writing style:

- Since I'm also a blogger, I actually get a lot of practice writing shorter pieces that are all wrapped up at the end.
- I'm attracted to the kinds of writing exercises where you end up writing a whole lot about nothing. I'm very good at coming up with a funny, last-minute idea about almost anything—a box of crayons, a sitcom I've just watched, Facebook, a pair of shoes. Anything.
- I don't think my pieces could stand on their own. While I'm good at writing shorter pieces that end neatly, they tend to be a little bit quirky. I would need to find some sort of thread that pulls them together.

STEP #2:
Examine Your Ultimate Memoir List

Sometimes it can be difficult to get a fantastic idea that lives in your head onto paper. When writing a memoir, all sorts of things can get in the way—emotions, anger, memories, etc. That's why it can be incredibly helpful to simply make a list of all of the elements of that picture-perfect memoir, the one that currently exists only in your head. Keep in mind that you can create your list in any way that works for you. Feel free to list adjectives, names of other memoirs, names of friends you want to include, events that must be covered, etc. Whatever you need to do to create a picture of your memoir. By listing these elements, you'll be able to see whether or not you're headed in the right direction with structure. For instance, if I were to list the elements of my Ultimate Memoir, it would need to include the following characteristics:

1970s
classic rock
Stephen
bad clothing
Mrs. Laubenheimer
bullies
summer
ice cream cones
The Greendale Public Library
Ramona the Pest
walking to school through the woods
humor
quirky
fast-paced
upbeat
character-driven
playing outside
not fitting in
reading
colorful
A Girl Named Zippy
Stuffed . . . but without restaurants
grandma's house
Coke bottles

So, if I were struggling with the structure of my memoir, but after this list realized I had been forcing myself to write long, depressing passages about bleak Wisconsin winters—just because I'm from the Midwest and felt that this is what I was supposed to do, I might be gaining some clarity about what kind of style I'm more comfortable with. My ultimate memoir list might encourage me to start exploring how I can work my material into passages that are lighter, shorter, and might be more fun for me to write and for the reader to read as well.

STEP #3:
The Three Things You Don't Want to Do
Under Any Circumstances

This exercise should take you about thirty seconds. The idea of this quick list is that it is a gut reaction. There are always tasks we dread doing, even when it involves things we typically enjoy, right? Call me crazy, but I actually kind of enjoy cleaning my apartment. Weird right? But when it comes to cleaning the stove, changing the litter box (well, duh), and taking out the garbage, I'd rather sharpen pencils with my teeth. Ditto writing. I love personal essays, writing how-to stuff, and blogging. But I know my strengths and weaknesses, and I'm realistic about what my lifestyle allows me to do. I was able to pound out my "under no circumstances" list in about five seconds. My list looked like this:

UNDER NO CIRCUMSTANCES DO I WANT TO DO:

1) research
2) a year of anything
3) travel

That reinforces my structure right there, and also shows me that I'm not a good candidate for the kind of memoir that does any sort of exploration. If I were running a tab, I could say I'm beginning to get some very good clues about what kind of structure would work well for me and the kind of memoir I'd like to write. I'm obviously leaning toward more of a straight narrative. I'm clearly not going to go anywhere, study anything, or do any sort of "year in the life" kind of activity that would lend a clear cut structure to my story.

I'm not going to have a calendar year, travel year, or season to lean on. Luckily my preset parameters will help me get started, but how will I structure all of that material and get from point A to point B? I'm doing these exercises just like you are, so I'm keeping a list, and am going to see what kind of structure ideas I come up with after completing all of the exercises. I have some ideas, but still have a ways to go before I start to get a clear picture.

STEP #4:

List Five New Things You Bring to the Table

This can seem tricky, but it can also help shine light on your memoir's finest features and can make the difference between your book coming off as just another travel memoir and an editor or agent being able to pick up on a truly unique aspect of your work. This exercise requires checking your ego at the door. This can be hard for some of us, but it's important that you be strong and confident when doing this particular exercise. You also need to be as creative and imaginative as possible. Be prepared to face some possible changes, too. Many writers have started off writing a book about one thing, only to find out that deep in their soul, they were truly meant to write about something different. This doesn't mean that these writers scrapped entire projects and started over completely. Sometimes there is a seed of an idea that gets mentioned in the beginning of say, chapter two. This seed of an idea starts to grow bigger in chapter three, and the writer realizes somewhere along chapter four that this is getting pretty interesting, and the writer is finding he really enjoys writing about this idea and wants to explore it further. But should he do this? Because didn't he set out to write a book about X. In chapter five, this idea has blossomed. There is no more ignoring this idea. This idea is turning into *the* book.

Since dealing with structure means dealing with framework and other technical aspects of your books, it presents a good opportunity for fine-tuning and adjustment. Your ideas are laid out in a blueprint just as if you were building a house. If there is something that doesn't work, or if you like the idea of expanding a certain area, it's during the blueprint stage where it's easiest to make changes. It's much more complicated and a lot more frustrating once your contractor has already started putting up walls. So the five new things you bring to the table are meant to make you take a closer look at anything truly unique, that you might really want to write about but are afraid to, strengths that you might be too chicken to tout, or cool things about you or your story that you're plain worried people will think are just dumb.

Here's what I came up with:

1) I am really good at writing funny stuff.
2) I can write short, succinct pieces.
3) I can capture time, character, place, etc.
4) I have a fun down-to-earth, Midwestern sensibility.
5) I've had the same best friend since I was four years old and we both moved out of Wisconsin to New York City.

I kid you not when I say that this is sometimes how bestsellers are born! It's important to listen to those tiny voices—and to look for clues that are leading you in a slightly different, but much more interesting, direction. Don't panic if you have to add something crazy onto your list. You'll see that my number five was that I've had the same best friend since I was four years old. We lived across the street from each other, and also lived next door to each other for several years in New York City. We both still live here and see each other all the time. Why did I add this? I looked over my "ultimate memoir list" and realized that he was with me when I experienced almost every single thing on that list. So maybe this is a hint that my memoir would be heavily weighted toward friendship? How might this also influence my structure?

STEP #5:

What Is a Narrative Thread and Why Do I Need One?

Narrative thread is basically a fancy term for whatever it is you use to hold all of the pieces of your story together. It's the element that can be found uniting each chapter to the next, adding cohesion and consistency to even the wackiest of stories. The narrative thread is also the missing element in a book of personal essays. You might be thinking, "Fine with me! I'll just call my manuscript a work of personal essays and be done with it." I would urge you to think twice about that. If you are chickening out on this endeavor because you aren't sure what your narrative thread is, then I'm led to believe you may have an issue in the cohesion department. Don't fool yourself into thinking essay collections lack cohesion. Sloane Crosly's delightful *I Was Told There'd Be Cake* was not just a bunch of pages with a cover slapped on it. Thought was put into the order and placement of each of those stories. Ditto David Sedaris and Laurie Notaro. An essay collection is not the easy out you might think it is. It's just different.

With memoir, narrative thread can actually give the writer quite a bit of flexibility. If you look at the examples I cited earlier on—Kirk Read's adolescence provided a simple narrative thread, while Patricia Pearson's investigation into anxiety provided one that was more complex. Her search for answers—to both her struggles, and those of other cultures—provided a very clear and easy to follow narrative thread. Had she suddenly started writing about the complications of heart disease in chapter four, I'm sure her editor would have made sure she had gotten back on track with her narrative. *Girls of Tender Age* has a clear narrative thread: the author's story of growing up, combined with Malm's story of becoming an increasingly dangerous predator. At no point does she completely switch to the political scene of Hartford in 1956.

Anything and everything she writes about supports her story and follows her narrative thread. So I hope that you've already answered the question, "Do I need a narrative thread?" with a very loud *yes!* Remember your narrative thread will keep your story moving forward, on point, and most importantly, will ensure it makes sense!

> **REALITY CHECK:** *If you're thinking of twisting your narrative thread in a certain direction to specifically follow a "trend," I'm here to tell you that once something is a trend in book publishing, it's already too late to jump on that bandwagon, no matter how trendy said wagon may be. Once you secure a publisher, it takes **at least** nine months to produce a book. The chances of that trend still being desirable by the time your book is finished is slim. You're much better off using your energies to come up with an innovative new structure or narrative thread than to waste anyone's time copying a trend that people in publishing are likely already sick of. If something lands in my mailbox promising to be the next* Marley & Me *or* The Tender Bar, *chances are it goes right in the trash.*

STEP #6:
What Does Your Blueprint Look Like?

Take a look at your notes from all five steps and look at the picture that's starting to develop. Are there clues in each section that are helping you see what your memoir's blueprint should look like? By looking at your strengths, weaknesses, and preferences and by examining your comfort zones, you should be able to see what kind of blueprint makes sense for your personal story. This memoir is going to be with you for a very long time, so it is incredibly important that you feel at ease with its framework. If you are most relaxed on a plump sofa absolutely covered with cushions, you shouldn't buy an ultra modern leather sofa that is hard and sleek. You'll never be satisfied. You'll be frustrated, uncomfortable, and maybe you'll just decide to get rid of the sofa all together. Don't make the same mistake with your life story. If you enjoy writing with a folktale-like quality and would like to use this trait to write about your life growing up in the projects of Brooklyn but feel pressured to "follow a trend," and you're thinking a "year in the life" memoir about your first year on Wall Street is more marketable, think twice about how well you'll do with it if you're not following your heart. You're doing yourself a disservice. Will you be able to pull off your heartfelt work and get it published? Who knows? Is it worth a try? Yes.

To see what the steps say about you, start to make a list of what you've learned and start looking for elements about your writing style or preferences that you might not have noticed before. Did you learn something about the length of work you prefer? Or did your ultimate memoir list point you in a different direction that you initially expected? Did something from your "five new things" list pull up a most unexpected surprise? The idea here is to combine some notes from what you just did with some of the other elements we've worked out in previous chapters. You'll want to incorporate your parameters and hook into this section to complete your blueprint.

Here's what my blueprint looks like:

PAULA'S WRITING STYLE & STRENGTHS, A QUICK SUMMARY

- shorter pieces, sharp and tight style
- funny, quirky, aim to make people laugh, lighthearted
- no year in the life, research, or travel
- What do I bring to the table? Midwestern sensibility, humor, best friend story.

BLUEPRINT

THEME

A funny memoir focusing on the friendship of two unlikely best friends and the unusual strength of their relationship.

HOOK

Paula and her best friend, Stephen, met in their Wisconsin suburb the summer before they entered the first grade. They never imagined that the bonding they did over Saturday morning cartoons, walks to school, taunting from various bullies, and summers of letter writing while Stephen was away with his family would result in a lifelong bond that continues over thirty years later. Their friendship has endured the loss of a parent, recovery from alcoholism, two moves to New York City, and countless breakups with men. Thankfully, they no longer have to worry about bullies.

FIRST PARAMETER

Meeting Stephen the day I moved into my house on Balsam Court in Greendale, Wisconsin.

LAST PARAMETER

When Stephen moves to Long Island, and we realize we don't always have to live within 100 feet of the other.

Paula's Narrative Thread

Because I realized that this book is very much about friendship (which I didn't really know until I did the "five things" exercise), there are a number of ways I could handle my narrative thread. Stephen and I wrote letters starting when we were in about fourth grade. If we still had them, and if he was okay with it of course, it could be an option to start chapters with letters. But how helpful can letters from nine year olds be? Letters are probably better left to older people. One interesting thing about my friendship with Stephen was that he went away to his family's vacation house each summer, but then permanently moved there when we were in the fourth grade. Moving is a big theme with us. Therefore, it might make sense to divide it into sections depending on where we were living. I also like the idea of starting each chapter off with a season, because seasons also played a big part in our relationship. Stephen would return every fall but go away every summer. And if you've ever spent a winter in the Midwest, you know it's rough.

A rough sketch of my narrative thread looks like this:

Chapter one, Fall 1976
Chapter two, Winter
Chapter three, Spring
Chapter four, Summer
Chapter five, Fall 1977

And so on. Obviously, to make my chapters more interesting I can add an actual title or a tagline of some sort. Remember, this is just my blueprint and not a final outline. This is to help me see where I'm going and to get me writing. But I agree that the seasonal aspect works and feels comfortable. You may decide to follow a more year in the life structure, which is more clean cut. Or maybe your story can work with a very unique and unusual structure, which is always fun and exciting. Whatever you select, just make sure that it works well with your story and your writing style. If you meet those criteria and you're communicating the story to your reader in a readable but interesting way as a result, then you can be sure that your blueprint has done its job.

MEMOIRISTS SHARE THEIR FAVORITE MEMOIRS

MELISSA HOUTTE, AUTHOR OF *ALLIGATORS, OLD MINK & NEW MONEY*

Don't Let's Go to the Dogs Tonight by Alexandra Fuller. This book is both shocking and breathtaking, and as intimate as it is global. With the story of one family's often ugly life in Rhodesia, I was reminded just how sheltered my own life had been.

RECOMMENDED READING

MEMOIRS WITH MEMORABLE STRUCTURES

Stuffed: Adventures of a Restaurant Family by Patricia Volk

Julie and Julia: 365 Days, 524 Recipes, 1 Tiny Apartment Kitchen by Julie Powell

How to Stop Time: Heroin From A to Z by Ann Marlowe

Summer at Tiffany by Marjorie Hart

The Hungry Ocean: A Swordboat Captain's Journey by Linda Greenlaw

How I Learned to Snap: A Small Town Coming-of-Age & Coming-Out Story by Kirk Read

The Happiness Project or, Why I Spent a Year Trying to Sing in the Morning, Clean My Closets, Fight Right, Read Aristotle, and Generally Have More Fun by Gretchen Rubin

A Likely Story: One Summer With Lillian Hellman by Rosemary Mahoney

Waiting For Daisy: A Tale of Two Continents, Three Religions, Five Infertility Doctors, an Oscar, an Atomic Bomb, a Romantic Night, and One Woman's Quest to Become a Mother by Peggy Orenstein

Encyclopedia of an Ordinary Life by Amy Krouse Rosenthal

TOOL #2:
Voice—How to Find It, How to Use It

I was approaching the dark side of my twenties, but I shook like a rattle, still felt like a teenager with fire ants in my Calvins. The big move to Minneapolis had provoked some psychological agita, and I felt like I had been handed a final opportunity to raise some serious heck-ola without facing grown up consequences. I say "final" because I had always been a pretty well-behaved human female. Evidence: I'd never ridden on a motorcycle, not even a weak Japanese one. I'd never gotten knocked up or vacuum-aspirated. I'd received every available Catholic sacrament with the exception of matrimony and last rites. I'd completed college in eight tidy semesters (one nervous break-down per). I'd never thrown a glad of Delirium Tremens in anyone's face. I'd never even five-fingered a lipstick at the Ben Franklin. I was a drag, baby. My mid-twenties crisis weighted my gut like a cosmic double cheeseburger. I guess that's one reason I ended up half naked at the Skyway Lounge."

—from *Candy Girl* by DIABLO CODY

When I received a manuscript called *Candy Girl* by a former stripper named Diablo Cody, I wasn't too interested based on the subject matter alone. Stripping had been covered before (no pun intended), and I didn't think the author was likely to add much to an already crowded market. But then there was *the voice*. After just one paragraph, I was a) completely convinced that stripping was the solution to all of her problems, b) laughing uncontrollably, and c) definitely interested in being along for the entire ride, or at least 250-plus pages. This is what "voice" is all about.

WHAT IS VOICE?

"Voice" is what gives personality and originality to a work; it's almost like your book's fingerprint—only the author can give a book it's own voice and style. It's that special something that makes one particular book on stripping hilarious and uplifting while another might be just plain depressing. Voice can make a book about almost any topic fascinating, from teaching to cattle ranching, and it can make the most wretched of circumstances uplifting. Your voice is also a uniting element. It's the glue that ties everything together. The structure you choose to build your memoir on, your setting, your story, all of these elements are tied together by the voice you use. It's what introduces all of these elements to the reader. Think of your memoir's voice as your book's personality. We won't know if your memoir is quirky, funny, semi tragic, and ultimately uplifting unless your voice lets us know it is. Frank McCourt's childhood in *Angela's Ashes* and Haven Kimmel's childhood in *A Girl Named Zippy* have a completely different feel, even if on some level they are both tragic in their own right. This is because each of these authors has a completely different voice, and they use it to relay their stories in different manners.

> **REALITY CHECK:** *What this chapter is not about is trying to be something you're not. We can't all be the next Diablo Cody or Augusten Burroughs, but ultimately, the world would be a pretty dull place if we all wrote just like they did. While you might feel tempted to emulate your favorite writers,* don't do it. *Developing an authentic voice is going to help you create a readable memoir, while a poor copy of something that already exists is going to land your manuscript in the trash.*

But does everyone have a voice? The answer, luckily, is YES—everyone has a voice. But no, not all voices are created equal. That's okay.

This chapter is about figuring out what your voice sounds like, and working effectively with what you've got. Every voice has its own strengths, and we're going to figure out what those are and work together to maximize them in your memoir.

What Exactly Makes a Voice Good?

"She's got a great voice," is something you hear in book publishing I would bet as much as you do on the set of *American Idol*. Agents and editors are always on the lookout for a great new "voice"—and there is nothing more exciting than looking at the first page of a manuscript and having that special, one-of-a-kind voice pop right off of the page. But what exactly *is* a voice? And what makes a good one? It's definitely not the easiest thing to describe, but an author's voice consists of the patterns, habits, and language she uses, and how, when put together, they create a style that is that particular author's alone. I always tell my authors that if they're writing at their best, and they sent me their manuscript without putting their name on it (which by the way, I would *never* recommend doing unless you wanted your agent to be incredibly annoyed with you), that I should be able to tell whether it's the work of writer X or writer Z, if they are using their carefully crafted and well-honed voices. So what elements make up a good voice? A good voice should aim to do the following:

- add style and energy to the writing
- present prose in a manner that is unique, interesting, and readable
- enhance the story being told, not distract from the events taking place
- engage and excite the reader
- relay the events taking place with appropriate emotion

Using your voice means having the confidence and courage to let your writing style shine. This takes loads of practice, diligence, and in some cases, I would argue, "un-learning" some of the very things you spent years learning about throughout your education.

> **QUICK TIP:** *Don't be afraid of weird quirky details, as it's often the quirky details that are the most memorable and add life and color to your story. For instance, in* Running With Scissors, *Augusten Burroughs could have easily thought, "Hey, wow, it's really weird that I used to be so into having shiny pennies that I would BOIL THEM," and decided to leave that detail out of his story. Ultimately, that tidbit turned out to be funny and a great insight into what Burroughs's personality was like as a child. Had he been worried that such a detail would be dismissed as boring, he would have missed a great opportunity to show off both his voice and his personality when he was a kid.*

Learning to Break the Rules Correctly

Lest every English teacher on the face of the planet come after me, please note that grammar and punctuation are incredibly important and the English language should be used properly and with respect. So let me start out by saying that my "breaking the rules correctly" method is by no means a substitute for not knowing the rules in the first place. I assure you that any agent or editor will *immediately* know the difference between a writer who is artfully playing with language and someone who just plain doesn't have a clue what they're doing. Furthermore, there are so many wonderful books and online tools that there is no excuse for not having a decent understanding of grammar and punctuation. Ditto spelling. I will confess right now that I am positively wretched with spelling, and I'm not exactly terrific with punctuation either. It's tricky stuff sometimes! But I am never too far from my dictionary, and I have my favorite online tools that I refer to whenever I'm in doubt. I highly recommend you do the same.

So what do I mean by "breaking the rules correctly" anyway? Oxymoron anyone? I have found that sometimes writers feel a need to be correct, and this need to conform to the picture-perfect sentence structure we learned about in grade school can really be an obstacle when it comes to finding your voice. If a writer spends too much energy focusing on creating the perfect sounding sentence, the writing is often completely devoid of any kind of life or energy that makes the prose worth reading. What you end up with, while *correct*, is often flat and dull. What are some signs that you might need to let loose and break a few rules?

- constantly self-editing as you write
- using too many or too few words, i.e., feeling you need to have a specific number of adjectives or verbs to properly describe something
- wanting to write the way you sound in your head, but worry that the way you sound in your head is "wrong"
- not being able to translate the voice you envision onto paper

Feeling a need to write correctly is common, and believe me, this need springs from good instincts! There are some exercises later in this chapter to help break down some of these barriers and to help you sort out when it is absolutely necessary to follow the rules, and when it might be okay to toss a few out the window. With practice and patience, you'll be safely and comfortably following your own set of rules in no time at all. For now, if finding your voice has been an issue, and you know you've been spending time agonizing over the structure of each and every sentence you write, know that these exercises might be particularly helpful to you, and you just may have discovered one of the major reasons why you've had trouble using your authentic voice. Hang in there, you'll get it.

A QUICK WORD ABOUT POV

Before we get to work on that fabulous voice of yours, there are a few things I should mention. It's a common mistake to confuse "voice" with "point of view." For our purposes, when I'm referring to voice, please know that I'm not talking about which point of view your story is being told from. I'm talking about they *way* you're telling your story, or how you use your own unique writing talents to put your personal stamp on your work. That being said, point of view is important, and it certainly plays a role in getting your story across. If you're anything like me, you haven't had a reason to think about point of view since ninth grade English class, which feels like ages ago. Point of view basically refers to the position from which your memoir will be told. To refresh your memory, following is an example of each type of point of view:

First Person

> Most mornings I got out of bed and went to the refrigerator to see how my mother was feeling. You could tell instantly just by opening the refrigerator. One day in 1960 I found a whole suckling pig staring at me. I jumped back and slammed the door, hard.
>
> —*Tender at the Bone* by RUTH REICHL

First Person Plural

> We ached to impress our grandfather—or, at least, not to humiliate ourselves. On our turn, if there was no obvious play, we'd glance uncertainly about the table, hoping for a hint from him as to which shot we should attempt.
>
> —*The Big House* by GEORGE HOWE COLT

Second Person

> You're reading a fairy tale in your evening Italian class when you come across this phrase. You think you know what it means, since the sea

princess says it after her one true love abandons her, but you ask the teacher anyway.

—An Italian Affair by LAURA FRASER

Third Person

My mother enjoyed claiming direct descent from Genghis Khan. Having asserted that one eighth of her blood was Tartar and only seven eighths of it 'ordinary Russian,' with a panache that no one else could have pulled off she proceeded to drop a few names in the chronology of our lineage: Kublai Khan, Tamer lane, and then the great Mogul monarch Babur, from whose favorite Kirghiz concubine my great-grandmother was descended, and voilà!, our ancestry was established.

You couldn't have argued the point with her, for in her quest for dramatic effect Tatiana du Plessix Liberman would have set all of human history on its head. Besides, you mightn't have dared to risk a showdown: in her prime, she was five feet nine and a half inches tall and 140 pounds in weight, and the majesty of her presence, the very nearsighted, chestnut-hued, indeed Asiatic eyes that fixed you with a brutally critical gaze through blue-tinted bifocals, had the psychic impact of a can of Mace.

—Them: A Memoir of Parents by FRANCINE DU PLESSIX GREY

Obviously, since you're dealing with memoir, you're most likely going to be dealing with a first person narrative. But, every once in awhile, some very clever writer does figure out a way to make the second person work for a memoir. One particularly effective example of this is Laura Fraser's *An Italian Affair*, which I mentioned in the above example. This memoir follows the author to Italy after a painful breakup. Notice how her use of the second person creates an extra powerful, gut-wrenching effect. I admit that the first time I read *An Italian Affair* I was in tears before I finished the prologue:

Mi hai spaccato il cuore.

You're reading a fairy tale in your evening Italian class when you come across this phrase. You think you know what it means, since the sea princess says it after her one true love abandons her, but you ask the teacher anyway.

> *"You have broken my heart," he says, and he makes a slashing motion diagonally across his dark blue sweater. "You have cloven it in two."*
> *Mi hai spaccato il cuore.*
> *The phrase plays over and over in your mind, and the words in front of you blur. You can see your husband's face with his dark, wild eyebrows, and you whisper the phrase to hint, Mi hai spaccato il cuore. You say it to plead with him, to make him stay, and then you say it with heat, a wronged Sicilian fishwife with a dagger in her hand. But he doesn't understand, he doesn't speak Italian; you shared so many things in your marriage, but Italy was all yours.*

Fraser's use of the second person makes the reader feel that she is, in fact, experiencing this loss right alongside the author, or worse, in place of! Believe me, it isn't easy to sustain the second person throughout an entire book—and it's pretty astonishing that she manages to pull it off—but that's what finding your voice is all about, knowing what works right for you, what you're capable of, what works right for your story, and knowing how to implement it. When you find your voice and become comfortable using it, you are giving your memoir a great gift.

COMMON VOICE STUMBLING BLOCKS

Just the Facts Ma'am

Have you ever been seated next to someone at a dinner party who was especially difficult to make conversation with? No matter what you did, you just couldn't get a feel for this person? Their likes or dislikes? Where they came from, what they did for a living, if they preferred dogs over cats, etc.? You ask them, "Hey, how do you know *insert name of hostess here?*" and all you get back is "College." Not a hint of personality couched within some additional juicy information, like, "Oh, we met in college when we were both on parole for diamond smuggling." All attempts to create conversation are met with "yes" or "no" answers, and while this guy may very well be a world famous NASCAR driver or a leading expert in stem cell research, unless he's capable of communicating the information, you're going to give up and start talking to the person on the other side of you.

I can't tell you how many promising (and by promising, I mean the author has a very interesting story to tell) memoirs I've received, where I actually think "Wow, if this is as good as it sounds, it could be HUGE!"—only to be hugely *disappointed* by the utter lack of voice. Instead of finding an interesting way to relay their story, many authors fall prey to the "just the facts ma'am" syndrome, where they focus so much energy on telling their story and getting all the facts out on the page that they completely forget about the importance of voice—which is where all the storytelling comes in. Worried you might be falling into the "just the facts" trap?

Ask yourself the following questions:

1. Am I more focused on getting my story straight, i.e., what happened when, than I am about describing how things felt and looked? Am I more focused on facts than an overall picture?
2. Is my manuscript devoid of emotional reactions to the events I am describing?
3. Am I feeling hesitant or nervous about letting my personality show in my memoir?

All Voice and No Substance. . .

We've all met those writers who could write a beautiful paragraph about a broken pencil or a single strand of grass. Then there are the writers who can write something that is laugh out loud funny, but when you really think about the content of what they've written, they've managed to write an entire story about a dead goldfish. Yes, that's what's known as raw talent. While it does exist, it is rare. Please believe me, even those super gifted people who can write mind-blowing prose about their new toothbrush still have to create marketable and readable works, and that means there has to be an actual narrative buried within their genius musings about nothing. In the age of blogging and with the popularity of essays by writers, such as David Sedaris and Laurie Notaro, it can be easy to think you can let your voice do all the work and let your story take the backseat. While I will admit to being a huge believer that a special voice can breathe new life into a tired subject, don't fool yourself into thinking a strong voice can make up for a weak story.

If you answer *yes* to the following questions, you may be relying on that pithy little voice of yours for too much.

1. When asked what your memoir is about, you end up listing several completely disjointed and totally unrelated themes that you can't tie together.
2. You've decided you'll "work on your voice first" and worry about your narrative later.
3. You've "found your voice," but have been forced to start over using several different stories a few times.
4. After several attempts, you admit you "just don't know."

While it's important (and of course fun) to have an interesting or quirky voice, I dare say it's time to borrow a phrase from various MFA programs across the country and spend a moment talking about "authenticity." When I refer to authenticity, to some extent, I'm referring to whether or not you want to sound like a pretentious jerk. And do you? If you write perfectly lovely prose, there is no need to try to mess with it to the point where it sounds so edgy that your wonderful memoir about spending a year herding sheep in rural Italy comes across like it was written by a member of the Hell's Angel's. And on the flip side, if you, in fact, *are* a member of the Hell's Angel's, go ahead and sound like one! A large part of "finding your voice" is finding the voice that suits you. Not only does it need to be readable, understandable, and interesting, but it needs to relate well to the person who is *actually writing it.* Just something to keep in mind. Let's look at some other examples of voice in recent memoirs. Be sure to keep the following ideas about voice in mind:

- How does the author's voice fit in with the story? Or does it provide an interesting contradiction?
- Technically, how does the author's voice come across? Long and flowing, short and to the point? Humorous? Poetic?
- How does the author use her voice to highlight particular portions of her story?
- Are their parts of my memoir that I could emphasize more using my voice?

BLACKBIRD BY JENNIFER LAUCK

In her memoir *Blackbird: A Childhood Lost and Found*, Jennifer Lauck recounts her childhood beginning from the perspective of a five-year-old girl who is in the position of having to do things a child should never have to do for a parent. I remember a very ordinary scene in the beginning of the book that was incredibly painful to read, mainly because it was told in the voice of a child. Had this story been told in Lauck's adult voice, it would have been sad of course, but frankly, it wouldn't have packed the same emotional punch, and I can't actually imagine that her book would have been as successful. Lauck is remembering her morning ritual with her chronically ill mother, who was usually bedridden when she wasn't in the hospital. Lauck was told to wait quietly until she heard her mother use the bathroom, and five-year-old Jenny always obeyed. She then prepared toast, just the way her mom liked it, made coffee, and served her mom in bed on a tray, hoping that today would be a "good day" and that her mom might be well enough to get out of the bed and sit on the sofa and read fashion magazines. As Lauck's mother's health worsens, her tasks come to include cleaning her catheter, washing soiled sheets, and doling out her countless medications. The memoir not only details her mother's death,

---

but also her father's, and finds Jennifer and her brother going from suburbia to the slums very quickly. Lauck's childhood voice is full of innocence, hope, love, and to some extent, of course, naiveté. It's a painful memoir to read at times, but the strength this young voice always manages to hold is truly amazing.

TRAVELING MERCIES: SOME THOUGHTS ON FAITH BY ANNE LAMOTT

Anne Lamott is, of course, the best-selling author of *Operating Instructions: A Journal of My Son's First Year* and *Bird by Bird: Some Instructions On Writing and Life* (which is super helpful for writers and a must read by the way). In *Traveling Mercies*, Lamott gets into her spiritual side, which is often hinted at in her other works. If you've read Lamott before, you know that her background has included some wild living, including bulimia, alcohol abuse—and when she was at her lowest, she became pregnant with her son and became a single mother. So, I couldn't help but wonder how her *"Hey, here's how I became a Christian"* book was going to come off. In typical Lamott style, it's full of quirkiness that she pulls off with ease. Check out this explanation Lamott gives as to why she has her now trademark dreadlocks:

> When I first started coming to this church, I wore my hair like I'd worn it for years, shoulder length and ringletty—or at any rate, ringletty if there was an absence of wind, rain or humidity. In the absence of weather, with a lot of mousse on hand, I could get it to fall just right so that it would not be too frizzy and upsetting—although "fall" is close. "Shellacked into the illusion of 'falling'" is even closer. Weather was the enemy. I would leave the house with bangs down to my eyebrows, moussed and frozen into place like the plastic sushi in the windows of Japanese restaurants, and after five minutes in the rain or humidity, I'd look like Ronald McDonald.
>
> Can you imagine the hopelessness of trying to love a spiritual life when you're secretly looking up at the skies for illumination or direction but to gauge, miserably, the odds of rain? Can you imagine how discouraging it was for me

to live in fear of weather, of drizzle of downpour? Because Christianity is *about* water: "Everyone that thirsteth, come ye to the waters." It's about baptism, for God's sake. It's about full immersion, about falling into something elemental and wet. Most of what we do in worldly life is geared toward our staying dry, looking good, not going under. But in baptism, in lakes and rain and tanks and fonts, you agree to do something that's a little sloppy because at the same time it's also bold, and absurd. It's about surrender, giving into all those things we can't control; its' a willingness to let go of balance and decorum and get drenched.

There is so much going on in just those two paragraphs, and it's all about the voice. Firstly, it's funny. Lamott is great with the self-deprecating humor, and the description of her shellacked hair and her desperate fear of rain is hilarious—but then the story takes another turn. While she stays on the theme of her hair, which we now know goes from Ronald McDonald level frizz-fest to dreads, the tone becomes much more serious. Lamott is able to use her voice to take the journey in a completely different direction, yet she manages to stay on the path. Her voice switches gears effortlessly from humor to a description of the joy of baptism—the joy of her faith. And it's clear within the weight of her voice that this is extraordinarily important to her, yet her tone remains fairly light—it never gets close to being preachy. It's quite a remarkable mix of emotions that her voice allows her to express in such a short passage. But then again, Lamott has been writing for years, and you don't become a best-selling novelist for nothing.

CANDY GIRL BY DIABLO CODY

In *Candy Girl* by Diablo Cody, a transplant from Chicago to the Twin Cities, finds herself working at an ad agency smack dab in the middle of a Midwestern winter. If you've ever experienced a Midwestern winter (I grew up in Wisconsin where it can be so cold, dark, and gray that sometimes the days just seem to blend one into the other), you know they can be rough. This manuscript landed on my desk, and the first sentence I read was "Nobody comes to

Minnesota to take their clothes off, at least as far as I know." It was followed by one of the most lively, but also most accurate descriptions of a Midwestern winter that I had ever read.

> *Here in the woebegone upper country, Jack Frost is a liberal, rangy sadist with ice crystals in his soul patch. Winter is the stuff of legend: stillborn, snow-choked, still as the ice floes on the ten thousand-odd lakes. The old mill cities are populated by generations of Scandinavian and German Lutherans, rugged soul hewn of blonde wood, good sense and Christ-love. The prevailing gestalt is one of wry survivalist humor and thermal underwear with pins still in the folds. Even the food is properly covered: Everyone's favorite supper is a gluey carbohydrate-rich concoction known simply as "hotdish" and served in community Pyrex. Minnesota is like a church basement with a leaky popcorn ceiling and a bingo caller who's afraid to amp things up past a whisper.*

Never mind that I knew the book was ultimately about stripping and the opening paragraph is initially focused elsewhere. If the author could make me shiver with a passage about a Minnesota winter on a sweltering summer day in New York City (August in New York is about as bad as winter in the Midwest, just in a different way), I knew that I had found something special. It was also an indication to me that the author was not out to tell a self-indulgent tale of her wilder days—but able to tell a more thoughtful, colorful, and completely new story about what it's like to be a stripper. It was clear to me that she could see the important details and would be able to relay a story to the reader that would be fascinating and could potentially be a huge seller.

MENNONITE IN A LITTLE BLACK DRESS: A MEMOIR OF GOING HOME BY RHODA JANZEN

This memoir definitely falls into the "truth *is* stranger than fiction" category. If this woman were writing fiction, her agent or editor would probably have had to tell her to tone down the drama a little bit. Here's the basic premise: Shortly after her fortieth birthday, as if that weren't traumatic enough, her husband of fifteen years left her *for another man.* Later that week she was seriously injured in a car accident, leaving her no choice but to move back in with her Mennonite parents. But life was tricky for Janzen even before her husband met another man on Gay.com. She suffered complications during a surgery that required her to wear a "pee bag," and we learn that this husband wasn't exactly award winning and those fifteen years were full of major ups and downs. But thankfully, going home to the Mennonites isn't about admitting defeat but starting anew.

Janzen's voice comes from not just her skill as a writer, but from her ability to translate the quirkiness of her family into passages that are funny but also sweet. A typical conversation with Janzen's mother on the topic of dating one of your own cousins or a pothead you went out with a couple of times looks something like this:

> One of the best things about my mother is that she will follow you anywhere, conversationally speaking. She will answer any question at all, the stranger the better. Naturally, I cannot resist asking her things that no normal person would accept.
>
> "Mom," I said, serious as a pulpit, "would you rather marry a pleasant pothead or your first cousin on a tractor? Both are associate professors," I hastened to add.
>
> "You marry your pothead if you like", she said generously, "as long as you wait a while. Let's say two years. But as for me and my house, we will serve the Lord."
>
> "Hey!" I said, indignant. "How do you know the pothead doesn't serve the Lord? As a matter of fact, this pothead does serve the Lord! He's more religious than I am." (I felt safe in asserting this because I had once heard the pothead softly singing "Amazing Grace".)
>
> "I think that the Lord appreciates a man on a tractor more than a man smoking marijuana in his pajamas," Mom said earnestly. "I know I do."

These scenes are laugh out loud funny, but because it is so clear that Janzen respects her family and shares a loving relationship with them despite their differences, you don't feel like you're laughing at them—not easy to pull off. She's able to use her voice to translate the scenes into something relatable, interesting, and funny.

IS YOUR VOICE STARING AT YOU RIGHT IN THE FACE?

Most writers have a voice they use that best shows off their writing style, whether it be in business, e-mails to a particular friend or a sister, postcards while traveling, journaling, or even Facebook status updates or Tweets. But when it comes to "writing," there is an annoying, pesky, internal critic that tells you "it's not good enough, it's too easy!"—and the voice goes AWOL. Writer Sloane Crosley whose book of essays *I Was Told There'd Be Cake* became a *New York Times* bestseller got her first essay published after sending a group e-mail to a bunch of friends. She had managed to lock herself out of both her old apartment and the new one she was moving into, and had to call on the services of the same locksmith twice in one day. Naturally, it helps to have friends who are editors at the *The Voice* as Crosley did, but a) you've got to start somewhere, b) you never know where you're going to make connections, and c) this chapter is about finding your voice—and she clearly found hers in that e-mail! I promise we'll talk more about making connections in chapter eleven.

 EXERCISE #1
WHERE ARE YOU MOST COMFORTABLE USING "YOUR VOICE?"

In one particular instance, I had a very funny client who had written a straight and very businesslike proposal that just wasn't what I had envisioned. His e-mails were always hilarious, as was his take on the subject. What happened? We decided he would try rewriting the proposal using his "e-mail voice." It worked! Sometimes it's just about finding the mode in which you are most comfortable.

I use this exercise frequently, and many of my clients who are published by major publishers have found this exercise incredibly helpful. Try paying attention every time you write for a couple of weeks. Letters, e-mails, postcards, Facebook posts, letters, cards, anything. Notice what feels right. What flows? Do you find yourself writing especially interesting and colorful accounts of your weekend to certain people? Is your journal work better at a certain place or at a certain time? You will eventually notice a pattern forming. Is there a voice that emerges in one particular format? How can you translate this voice into your memoir?

EXERCISE #2
COMMIT THE CROWD PLEASER TO PAPER

Is there a story you tell that always gets a laugh? Something that happened to you that's just too funny and it cracks people up every time you share it? Did something happen to you at some point in your life, and every time you tell the tale you have people on the edge of their seats? Have you been telling this story for years and getting the same positive result? Try committing this story to paper and see if you can get the same result. Don't worry if this story is about something hilarious that happened at the seventh grade dance and your memoir is about your travels in Africa. This exercise is about finding your voice, and if you're struggling to find it, it's always worth looking in places where you're getting positive reactions. As you commit your story to paper, think about what it is about your story that gets the positive reaction from people. Yes, it's partially about the story of course, but we all know that delivery is key. As you're writing your story, think about your delivery and what it is about how you tell the story that makes it work. How can you translate this to the page? Are their aspects of this "storytelling" that can translate to your writing voice?

EXERCISE #3
GO BACK IN TIME

While not everyone needs to tell the tale of their childhood from the perspective of a child, it can certainly be helpful to try to look at your story in a different light, and perhaps take a stab at writing it from a different angle. Remember, I'm not necessarily suggesting you scrap everything you have and start over, but if you need to loosen up and work on your voice, this may be a worthy exercise. Select a passage that's been giving you difficulty, and try to put yourself back into that place. Remember who you were then. What were things like? What were you feeling? What kind of person were you? What would the person you were then have sounded like? Try rewriting the passage from the perspective of the person you were then. See how it comes out. While this may or may not result in a new voice, it may help you loosen up or become more comfortable using your voice.

 EXERCISE #4

BANISH YOUR EVIL INNER CRITIC

In her inspiring and beautifully written memoir, *This Is Not the Story You Think It Is: A Season of Unlikely Happiness*, Laura Munson is dealing with some heavy stuff, including a messed-up husband who dared utter the words "I don't think I love you anymore." Knowing there was a damn good chance he didn't mean it, the author stuck to her original plan, which was to "take responsibility for her own happiness." And who was one of the biggest obstacles in all of this? Her evil imaginary twin "Shelia." This is how Munson describes Shelia's arrival:

> *"Apparently the planets of Hell that live inside me were aligned just so the night before, and tah-dah—regardless of therapy, she's managed to ride in on her broomstick like Samantha's brunette doppelganger, Serena on Bewitched."*

I dare say we all have known "a Shelia." That person that tells you "You're no good." "What you're doing is ridiculous-silly-awful-and-will-never-amount-to-anything." I love that Munson took control of her inner demon by naming her and therefore making it easier to tell her off! Okay, that might sound kind of crazy, but the next time you hear yourself saying "I suck." Think about it.

This exercise is especially helpful for those of us who are plagued by the evil inner critic who shouts out, "Hey! You can't start a sentence with the word AND! Have you lost your mind! I don't care if you were in the middle of writing one of the best passages you've ever written. And while I'm at it, if you don't even know that, maybe you shouldn't be writing at all, and you should just give up because you suck!" Has this ever happened to you? Okay, maybe my inner-critic is slightly more dramatic (and mean) than yours, but most writers have one, and they can be a real pain in the ass. As I said earlier in the chapter, they can often get in the way of finding your voice, as they like to remind us about pesky things like the rules of grammar and punctuation, which can be really annoying when we've finally figured out how to write about a passage we've been stuck on for two months! So, I'm here to say that you should banish your inner critic. Do not allow them into your writing space. They are not welcome.

STEP #1

The first thing you need to do is begin practicing freestyle writing. Conjure up your inner café society poet, grab your computer or notebook, and just let yourself write about whatever you want without giving a single care to what Margaret or James thinks. Write about absolutely whatever you want for a minimum of fifteen minutes. Do not worry about the quality of your writing; you're just practicing getting the words flowing. If the idea of writing about whatever you want freaks you out (I know it does me. I like direction!) consider the following:

Write about where you are right now.
Write about your favorite room in your home.
Write about your best childhood friend.
Write about your greatest fear.
Write about your biggest regret.
Write about your favorite food.
Write about family vacations.

Write for fifteen minutes each day for a week—minimum. Do this for additional weeks if you're still stressing out over what you're writing. The idea is to just get the words flowing. Once you're feeling more comfortable you're ready for:

STEP #2

You're ready to try this with your actual memoir. Decide which section of your manuscript you want to work on and make a commitment to yourself that you will not criticize or reread what you're writing while you write, and you will not self-edit. Make a commitment to write a certain number of pages during a specific period of time (you set the pages and timeframe). Be reasonable: Don't set crazy goals but do challenge yourself. Work this way until you feel the words flying out, but your inner critic is quiet. Will your prose be perfect the first round? No! Maybe not even the second time! But I guarantee you that it will never be perfect if you never give yourself a chance to actually get it on the paper in the first place!

RECOMMENDED READING

MEMOIRS WITH GREAT VOICE

Mennonite in a Little Black Dress by Rhoda Janzen

Candy Girl by Diablo Cody

Running With Scissors by Augusten Burroughs

A Girl Named Zippy by Haven Kimmel

An Italian Affair by Laura Fraser

Blackbird by Jennifer Lauck

Kitchen Confidential by Anthony Bourdain

Julie and Julia by Julie Powell

Alligators, Old Mink & New Money by Alison and Melissa Houtte

How I Learned to Snap by Kirk Read

A Brief History of Anxiety: Yours and Mine by Patricia Pearson

Traveling Mercies by Anne Lamott

Drinking: A Love Story by Caroline Knapp

Slackjaw by Jim Knipfel

This Is Not the Story You Think It Is: A Season of Unlikley Happiness by Laura Munson

CHAPTER SIX

TOOLS #3-6:
Dialogue & Pacing, Killer First Paragraphs, and Awful First Drafts

I've been anticipating writing this section with equal amounts of excitement and dread. That's because writing good dialogue is so hard that I'm terrified I won't be able to do a good job of explaining it properly, but also because I've come across so much bad dialogue in manuscripts over the years that I was quite looking forward to writing a really excellent example of *really bad dialogue* for you. So without further ado:

> "I don't care what you think anymore!!!!" Marcia shouted.
> "I'm sick of the lies!!!!"
> "NO!!!" I said.
> "Get out of my life you scoundrel!!!!" Marcia exclaimed loudly.
> "I've had enough!" I said.

That was actually rather enjoyable to do, and I hope you're cringing, because that my friends, is bad dialogue. Allow me to extrapolate on a point-by-point basis:

1) Exclamation marks. There is a time and place for them, and I assure you the time and place for them is not in every sentence you write. Sure, I like to toss one in every now and then, but it's your job as a writer to get the point across with your words as much as possible, and NOT! With your punctua-

tion!!!!!!! See what I mean? Furthermore, when you do find an appropriate place to use an exclamation point, I assure you, one is sufficient.

2) Notice how I'm beating a dead horse by commenting on my own awful dialogue. Seriously? Do I really need to add "Marcia shouted?" I mean, yeah, we get the point. This is just much too obvious a way to write about a heated conversation. What we've got here is one giant cliché.

3) If that weren't enough, the annoying festival of exclamation points, self-commentary, and massive clichés continues.

4) And yes, while you do want to stretch a bit and toss in some unusual words whenever possible, be realistic about it. I ask you, when is the last time you heard someone say "you scoundrel?" There is a difference between being creative and just being "out there."

So, what's the proper way to go about this? My rule is to not overthink dialogue and try to sound as natural as possible. If you were to read my piece of writing out loud, you would realize that you sound like something from a daily soap opera or a 1930s radio drama. And trust me, that's just not good.

Here are a few things to keep in mind when working on your dialogue:

1) Listen to conversations. How can you translate them to the page in a way that is natural but not boring?

2) Don't let the conversation go on for too long. Remember that as the narrator, you can come back in to break up the dialogue with explanation or action. Too much dialogue in a memoir is going to feel awkward and suspicious. Dialogue in memoirs is meant to give flavor and a sense of what was happening. It is not meant to give a play-by-play account of what happened throughout your life story.

3) Avoid using "he said" and "she said" too frequently. Think about it, do you need to point out at all that he or she in fact said something at all? Or would it break your dialogue up nicely if you occasionally added a "he laughed" or "she snickered." Get playful, mix things up—just remember to keep it natural.

4) Read your dialogue out loud and ask yourself—does this sound normal?

5) Ask yourself if the portion of your memoir that you want to write in dialogue form would truly be better if written in dialogue form. In other words, do you really need to go there?

Dialogue for Memoir Writers: An Unusual Challenge

While I've just given you some really solid, basic, nuts-and-bolts advice about writing dialogue, there's one major glaring issue. What if I don't remember exactly what everyone said? How am I supposed to remember exactly what my third grade classmates said after I ruined the Christmas pageant? I can't even remember if my husband said, "Hey, you look pretty today." or "Wow, you look nice." Which was it? How is a memoir writer supposed to handle entire conversations? It is important to remember that it is unlikely that anyone is going to remember any conversation verbatim. The purpose of dialogue in memoir is to keep the story moving, inject energy into the story, and give the reader a better sense of the characters involved in the story. That being said, when selecting dialogue to use for your memoir, you'll want to draw on conversations that are meaningful to you, where you are more likely to have a clearer idea of overall framework of the conversation. It is also important to remember that conversations that take place in real life do not always translate well to the page. If a writer were to take a conversation and translate it verbatim, it would likely be wordy, suffer from poor pacing, and be somewhat disjointed to those of us who weren't actually there. While I'm not suggesting you embellish or put words into people's mouths, know that you do sometimes have to edit to make conversations work on the page.

Memoirs With Great Dialogue

In *Stuffed: Adventures of a Restaurant Family,* Patricia Volk tells the story of several generations of her family who owned a restaurant in New York City's garment district. Volk uses dialogue sparingly, but when she does, it's brilliant. She's able to determine when she should describe a particular situation and when it's best to let the characters, such as a colorful aunt or uncle, speak for themselves.

> It's a shocker, the Aunt Ruthie zinger. She loves you to death, she loves you so incredibly much you forget she zings. Then she zings. Sometimes I take a little vacation. I don't call. Then Aunt Ruthie phones, her voice wobbly, and says "why haven't I heard from you, my love?" and I'm over-come with missing her. Why does every encounter come with one poison dart? Is it the power to hurt that proves you still mean something to somebody? Is it a tic? Is this why the daughter-in-law I never met won't see her? Why the granddaughters don't call? Why has she never seen and held her great-grandchildren? How does Aunt Ruthie survive the hole in her heart where her family should be?
>
> "For the life of me"—Aunt Ruthie dabs her eyes with a hankie—"I don't know what I did. As God as my witness, you tell me darling. What on the face of this earth did I do?"
>
> This is the theme, the central gnawing conundrum of Aunt Ruthie's every waking day. How can people hate an old lady so much they won't let her see her own flesh and blood?
>
> Some things are breathtaking.
>
> To a child having trouble in school. "Your brother gets nothing but straight A's. What a pity you're having such difficulties darling."
>
> To an aunt with a weight problem: "Would you like a safety pin for that seam, my love? Fat people are so hard on clothes."
>
> To my mother whose hand-me-downs Aunt Ruthie depends on: "It cost me eleven fifty to fix the shoulders on the pink suit. Can you imagine, light of my life? Eleven dollars and fifty cents! It was out of fashion!"

Volk is lucky in that just about everything her entire family says is "a zinger." However, Volk is skilled at incorporating the dialogue into her narrative. In her story about Aunt Ruthie, she aptly describes Ruthie's dilemma: her cluelessness and "woe is me" attitude about why no one likes such a sweet little old lady, but then cleverly follows it up with three zingers that perfectly show that Ruthie is not quite as sweet as she claims to be. Had Volk used all dialogue in this section, it likely would have gotten old quickly, or the passage would have lost its humor, and just come off like the ranting of a mean, old lady. But combined with the author's commentary, it creates a perfect blend of explanation, color, and humor. The author ultimately is successful in using dialogue to achieve what she set out to do.

Jim Knipfel, author of *Slackjaw*, mixes his dialogue into his memoir in ways that intensify the experiences he's having—these experiences can include trying to get money from a social worker for being blind (which he is) but instead being pressured to go to AA, to being woken up in the middle of the afternoon by the paper he works for to see if he wants to fill in for the receptionist (even though the sales staff suspects he's a Nazi), to this episode with his "home survival genie" (the person who is teaching him how to navigate around his apartment now that he's losing his sight):

> A few hours after the Cane Lady left, my Home Survival genie rang the buzzer. Why he used regular doors and didn't just appear out of a puff of green smoke was a mystery. Probably too flashy for him. I went downstairs to let him in.
>
> "Hello, Mr. Knipfel! How are you today? How was your week?"
>
> "Oh, fine, fine." I was exhausted from the subway shenanigans. "How're you doing yourself, and how was your week?"
>
> "Oh, yes, fine. Fine!"
>
> "Well, I'm certainly glad to hear that."
>
> We entered the apartment, and he set straight to work.
>
> "Are you ready to cook a delicious casserole?" he said. "Let's start cooking!"

*I followed him into the kitchen, where he unpacked his various gro-
ceries. I already knew how to do most everything he was teaching me,
and had known for a long time. The problem was, I was usually too tired
and drunk when I got home at the end of the day to take the time to con-
coct a beef stew or whip up a soufflé. It was more feasible to throw a fro-
zen pizza in the oven and crack a beer. I told him this again and again,
but he wouldn't have any of it.*

"That's not home survival!" he would say.

Do you see the difference between this passage and the absolutely
horrible one I used to start off the chapter with? While yes, Knipfel is using exclamation points, and his dialogue might not be the
most natural sounding, because of the humor surrounding the
situation, it's clear that he's being tongue in cheek, and that his
dialogue is actually a pretty accurate depiction of the situation.
Also notice how he tosses in "I was exhausted from the subway
shenanigans," which is a reference to the previous passage, and an
indication that he's basically too tired to do anything but cheer-
fully banter with this guy (or outright mock him). So ultimately,
what could have come off as cliché and over-the-top dialogue is
actually really funny.

PACING YOUR MEMOIR

We all know that slow and steady wins the race, but writing a book
just isn't the same process, and a slow and steady memoir = BORING.
"Slow" and "steady" are just not words you want to see highlighted in
The New York Times Book Review. But then again, the truth of the
matter is, words like "fast-paced" or "thrilling"—and the phrase "on
the edge of your seat" just might not apply to your brand of memoir.
So how do you keep the pace moving along? How do you keep your
reader interested and engaged in your material if your life doesn't
resemble a Lee Child novel? While quality writing is obviously a big
help, paying close attention to the pacing of your memoir can also
make a difference.

Keep the following in mind to keep your prose flowing and your reader engaged:

1) Be honest with yourself at all times. While a passage is important to you, is it essential to the text overall? Or is it necessary to include as much as you have?
2) Constantly ask yourself if you are oversharing.
3) Ask yourself if your descriptions are too long. Do you need four pages to describe your childhood bedroom? Probably not.
4) If you have sorted out your key memory pieces and you've written fifty pages and have only included one of them, chances are, your memoir is going to be too long and you need to pick up the pace.

In her memoir, *Called Out of Darkness: A Spiritual Confession*, Anne Rice spends quite a bit of time describing the chapel where she worshipped in New Orleans as a child. I warn you to keep in mind that when you're as famous as Anne Rice, you are given some leeway, but I was charmed to see that even Anne Rice—who wrote a lengthy but extraordinarily beautiful description of the sky at dusk, incense, candles, the pews, the golden tabernacle, the plaster statues, and so forth, actually stops herself and lets the reader know she's aware of the indulgence in her description. She starts the very next chapter with the following words:

> Be relieved. I don't intend to describe eleven years of Catholic School in the same detail as I've described the world before school.

While she admits she didn't like school as much, she also seems well aware that to keep her story moving, she needs to *keep her story moving*. This isn't surprising coming from such a successful novelist as Anne Rice. After writing some of the most popular vampire novels to date, she knows a thing or two about keeping her audience happy.

When You Need to Slow Down

On the flip side, I've also worked with authors who don't seem to believe that there are elements to their stories that other people would actually want to read about. Their work, while hinting at interesting and exciting events, often feels superficial and lackluster. These authors present work that tends to feel more like an outline of a memoir than actual prose. This can certainly be a tricky problem to get over on your own, but I'll give you a few tips to see if those of you who need help in this department can't break the habit. If you suspect that you're suffering from a "who cares?" complex, I'm going to talk more about writing groups, writing partners, and some other options that will help you in chapter 10. But for now, ask yourself the following:

1) Am I able to write accurately and fully describe the events I uncovered in my key memory pieces? Sometimes writers who don't believe people will care about their stories just need to refer back to the key moments in their life to be reminded that their story matters.

2) Have I covered nearly everything I wanted to cover in a very short number of pages?

3) Is my memoir completely lacking any description, detail, or color?

4) When I mention other people in my memoir, am I simply mentioning them by name and omitting any details about them?

5) When I talk about an event that happened, am I talking about how that event made me feel or just describing it in a "just the facts ma'am" style?

If you are sensing that your memoir needs to be slowed down, and built up with color and detail, you can carefully read over what you have and ask yourself what's missing. Start a list of the sections that are lacking emotion, color, descriptions, and details. As always, there are some exercises at the end of this chapter to get you started.

FIRST IMPRESSIONS: CRAFTING THE PERFECT FIRST PARAGRAPH

You're probably wondering why I would bring up such an important topic as "crafting the perfect first paragraph this far into the book." I mean, if it was so important, why wouldn't I start with it? I mean, it is the first paragraph—would it not make sense for me to start my book with a discussion of *your* first paragraph? I totally see your point. Really I do, but the truth is, if we had this discussion on page one, I'm pretty sure you'd still be reading that page. Or you'd be so incredibly frustrated and angry that I caused you to obsess over your first paragraph at such great length, you would have thrown this book away and written to the publisher and demanded a refund. While I am a big believer that the first paragraph is extraordinarily important, it's tricky to pull off, and I don't think you're doing yourself a huge service by worrying about this right off the bat. It's an advanced maneuver. It would be kind of like getting in a car for your first driving lesson and saying to the instructor, "Hey! Let's start with parallel parking!" While creating a memorable and catchy first paragraph is by no means impossible, like parallel parking, it can be intimidating, and is best left until you've mastered some of the other basics. I think it's safe to say you've mastered those basics, and we're ready for this conversation.

What I'm about to tell you might prove to be controversial, but in my opinion, the first paragraph is one of the few things that will actually get me to read a manuscript. Obviously, the excellent, eye-catching first paragraph must be followed by other equally worthy paragraphs, but if a good query letter catches my attention, I'll take a peak at the first paragraph. If that first paragraph strikes me, I will keep reading. Have I missed out on good projects because some books didn't have great first paragraphs but had amazing paragraphs on page two? Possibly, but probably not. The authors I'm looking for know how to showcase their work in a good query letter and will carry that through on the first page of their manuscript. I'd also argue that a good first paragraph is as important as good flap copy and a well-designed book jacket. How many times have you looked at the first paragraph of a book at the book store and decided, based on the first paragraph alone, whether or not that book was a perfect match for you?

So how do you write a good first paragraph anyway? You want to grab your reader, hint at what's to come—all while showcasing that fabulous voice and style you've been working so hard to cultivate. Here is a rundown of guidelines for crafting a successful first paragraph:

- Showcase your voice and style.
- Indicate the setting of your story if that's essential, OR
- Indicate the situation your memoir is presenting.
- Hint at where the story is going to go.
- Make the tone of the opening line representative of the tone of the book.

SOME OF MY FAVORITE FIRST PARAGRAPHS

MANHATTAN, WHEN I WAS YOUNG
BY MARY CANTWELL

"It was a queer and sultry summer, the summer they electro-cuted the Rosenbergs. . ." That's how Sylvia Plath started The Bell Jar *and how I want to start this. Because that's the way I remember my first summer in New York, too.*

SLACKJAW BY JIM KNIPFEL

"SUICIDE HOTLINE?" the chipper young woman on the other end of the phone seemed to ask me when she answered.

When I dialed the phone, I had no idea what I was going to say. I hadn't thought that far ahead. What: "I'm going to open my veins. Now what the hell are you gonna do about it?" That wouldn't do. I get into trouble when I don't think about things beforehand. I've never been a good improviser. So instead of saying something moronic, I opted to say nothing at all."

RUNNING WITH SCISSORS
BY AUGUSTEN BURROUGHS

My mother is standing in the front of the bathroom mirror smelling polished and ready; like Jean Nate, Dippity Do and the waxy sweetness of lipstick. Her white, handgun shaped blow-dryer is lying on top of the wicker clothes hamper, tick-ing as it cools. She stands back and smoothes her hands down the front of her swirling, psychedelic Pucci dress, bit-ing the inside of her cheek. "Damn it," she says, "something isn't right."

STUFFED: ADVENTURES OF A RESTAURANT FAMILY
BY PATRICIA VOLK

Our hallway was the color of ballpark mustard. The living room was cocoa, my mother's wall-to-wall, iceberg green. The floor of the lobby was maroon-and-white terrazzo, like Genoa salami. When our elevator went self-service, the wood was replaced

> *by enameled walls that looked like Russian dressing, the lumpy*
> *pink kind our housekeeper, Mattie, made by lightly folding Hell-*
> *mann's mayonnaise into Heinz ketchup with a fork.*
>
> THIS IS NOT THE STORY YOU THINK IT IS
> BY LAURA MUNSON
>
> *At this moment in my life, I am strangely serene. In fact, I may*
> *have never felt more calm. Or more freed. Or more certain that*
> *these things owe themselves to a simple choice: to accept life*
> *as it is. Even and especially when it really fucking sucks. Even*
> *and especially if my husband left last night to go to the dump*
> *after announcing that he isn't sure he loves me anymore. . .*
> *and nine hours later, still hasn't come back.*

A FEW WORDS ON FIRST DRAFTS

The writer Anne Lamott is very smart and I highly recommend following her advice. One area about which she is particularly smart is the first draft. I am in total agreement with her about first drafts. In *Bird by Bird,* her fantastic book about writing, she has an entire chapter devoted to the subject titled "Shitty First Drafts" and it's definitely worth reading.

Every draft of every piece of writing is worth something. As an agent, I do hate telling writers that a manuscript they've been working on isn't working—or doesn't feel right. However, while not everything a writer works on ultimately "works" or leads to publication, it is *valuable.* You have to think of all writing as a workout. Athletes don't give it their all every single time they train for a marathon (seriously, I'm the last person on earth who should be making sports analogies, but I believe what I just said to be true). Why should everything a writer produces lead to publication? Why should everything a writer tries work at all? Don't be afraid to fail, experiment, and just generally play and mess around. That being said, if you go six months without knowing in your gut that you're making a sincere effort, you may have another problem that we'll discuss in chapter nine. Just know that the effort of producing, being imaginative and creative is important, and having huge expectations is not helpful. Don't expect the first draft of your memoir to be The Draft. It is normal to have to rework a manuscript many, many times. Brace yourself for lots of rewriting, redrafting, and sometimes just starting sections over. This is part of the process and part of what it means to be a writer. It does not mean you have failed or that the project you've originally conceived isn't going to work. It might mean, to borrow Lamott's phrase, that you've produced a "shitty first draft," or as I'd prefer to call it, a "semi-shitty first draft." It's to be expected. In fact, I'm not sure I know a single agent who has received a perfect first draft. It just doesn't happen. It goes against the natural law.

EXERCISES FOR DIALOGUE

In chapter five, we worked on your voice, and I hope some of that rubbed off on your dialogue as well. It's my feeling that if you're comfortable working with "your voice," chances are you're going to be able to use it to write good dialogue. Bad dialogue is often the result of overthinking things and not continuing to write in a natural fashion. If these points are kept in mind, writing dialogue will merely be an extension of your memoir, and hopefully you won't stop and think. "Oh my god ... I really need to write some dialogue ... Crap." You'll just do it naturally without even thinking about the fact that you're doing it. But if you're still not convinced that you can do it, try the following exercises. I promise that the next time you need to include a conversation in your memoir, it will be easier!

DIALOGUE EXERCISE #1: REWRITE THE CONVERSATION
We've all been in a situation where we're not proud of how we handled it—or we just didn't say what was truly on our minds. Now keep in mind that this exercise is about fictionalizing a conversation. Obvi-

ously, you're well aware that memoirs are nonfiction and if you plan to fictionalize the conversations in your memoir, you need to write a novel! For the purposes of this exercise and this exercise only, we're going to mess around with conversations just so we can see how to get them flowing. This is practice. While writing dialogue in a memoir, of course, you are basing your dialogue on memory—but you have yourself as the narrator as well. Before I complicate this exercise with ethics (see more on that in chapter fifteen), let me just explain what we're going to do here. Simply remember a conversation in which you wish you had said something that you didn't say. Remember how you felt during that conversation. Picture where you were, what the other person looked like, what they were doing, etc. Rewrite the conversation had you said what it is you would have liked to say. What does that conversation look like now?

DIALOGUE EXERCISE #2: TAKE IT PERSON BY PERSON

Just as it is important to establish your voice, it is also important to make sure that the voices you create for the different people in your memoirs are unique as well. This is a good opportunity to make sure that the dialogue in your memoir reflects this. Take some time to examine the dialogue you've written for each character. Is it consistent? Does each person sound unique? Make sure that you've developed a particular pattern, rhythm, and style for each of your characters. This is also a good opportunity to make sure you're not guilty of any clichés, excessive he said/she saids, or extra exclamation points.

EXERCISES FOR PACING

If you find that your manuscript is already more than one hundred pages long but you've only covered two of your key memory pieces, chances are you seriously need to pick up the pace. If your memoir isn't moving at a quick enough clip, you need to find out where you're getting stuck and why?

PACING EXERCISE #1: REVISIT THE PLACES YOU'VE BEEN AND EDIT, EDIT, EDIT

More often than not, when a book isn't moving, it's because the author is getting bogged down in too much description and is giving more detail about their teenage bedroom than anyone would ever want to know. Seriously, do we need to know the exact placement of every heavy metal poster you had in your room? Do you readers really want to hear about how long it took you to get that Van Halen poster hung just so? While some details like this are of course essential to creating the perfect picture of your life, it can be easy to get carried away and let the descriptions go on for far too long, or to include too many of them. Go through your manuscript and mark every place where you have a description of a place. It can be a room, a house, a vacation spot, a place in the country, a café—anything at all that warrants description. Be brutally honest with yourself about how much description is truly needed and start to decide which descriptions can be edited down and if there are some sections that can be cut completely. This process can be repeated with descriptions of events, emotional responses, and so forth. Remember, description is essential, but it can't take the place of actual story. If there are some passages that you would rather lose your right arm than edit, see if there are other sections you can take out or significantly cut down instead. Once you've gone through this process, read through your manuscript again and see if it starts to flow faster.

PACING EXERCISE #2: TAKE A LOOK AT WHAT'S MISSING

On the opposite end of the pacing problem spectrum, if you're flying through those memory pieces, but finding that you're running out of material, you're moving too quickly and you need to slow down. This issue is often the result of skimming through material and not really giving the reader any in-depth analysis or description of any of the situations you are writing about. To gain some traction and get some perspective on where you need to provide your reader with more information, try reading your manuscript and make a list of every single item you bring up that warrants description. On a separate piece of paper, write out three distinct things about the passage you are describing—things only you would know. Is it essential that your reader know these things? Do the things you listed make your descriptions more interesting and colorful? Go back through the descriptions in your memoir and see how many of them would benefit from having the items you listed added to their sections in the memoir. Sometimes you just need to step back and spend some extra time thinking about what makes a particular section special in order to really nail that description. If you continue to think about your writing this way, your manuscript will start to fill out nicely.

REALITY CHECK: *If after completing the pacing exercises your manuscript is still suffering from pacing issues, it's entirely possible that you just might need some extra help in the editing department. Don't panic, and remember my feelings about first drafts! We'll get into greater detail about writer's groups, classes, freelance editors, and those kinds of options in chapter ten.*

RECOMMENDED READING

BOOKS ON THE WRITING PROCESS

On Writing by Stephen King (bonus, it's *also* a memoir)

Bird by Bird: Some Instructions on Writing and Life by Anne Lamott

Writing Down the Bones: Freeing the Writer Within by Natalie Goldberg

If You Want to Write: A Book About Art, Independence and Spirit by Brenda Ueland

On Writing Well: The Classic Guide to Writing Nonfiction by William Zinsser

Eats, Shoots & Leaves: The No Tolerance Approach to Punctuation by Lynn Truss

The Elements of Style by William Strunk, Jr. and E.B. White

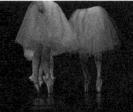

PART THREE

becoming the kind of writer publishers want

It's very easy to look at the career of a writer you admire and come up with a million reasons as to why you'll never meet their level of success. Okay, so maybe we all can't be as wildly popular as Elizabeth Gilbert or Augusten Burroughs, and I'm willing to admit that there are some things that fall out of our control. We can't necessarily predict the next publishing phenomenon (will it be cats or trips to China?). Seriously, please don't even try to guess. We all can't be the children of literary greats or publishing executives, not all of us can graduate from Ivy League schools—nor can all of us claim to come from big cities where the right connections might be easier to make. But we *can* take control over a few aspects of our careers that will make it more likely to become successfully published writers.

We've spent the first half of this book planning out our memoirs, carefully constructing our structure, and working on our voice—but what's the point of all this work if we end up with a product we're proud of but it's just going to languish in our desk drawer? Years of working with authors from all different backgrounds has taught me that one of the biggest differences between becoming a *published* author and one who just has a manuscript "in the drawer" is making an effort to do a few very specific things. Published authors obviously have talent, but more often than not, they make a sincere effort to carefully edit and consciously improve their work, educate themselves on the process of publishing and the media, they use their connections and if they don't have them they make them, and lastly they work hard to create a platform for themselves. I know you're a writer and that you want to spend your time writing. And it's important that writing remain the key focus here, but the bottom line is that publishing is a business and most authors do in fact want to reach an audience with their work. This portion of the book will help you become a more *valuable writer*. Once you've got the manuscript a publisher wants why not take it a step further and be *the author* publishers want? It's not easy, but there are steps you can take to make yourself valuable, marketable, and savvy.

CHAPTER SEVEN:

Setting Goals & Deadlines— and Why a Writer Without Either Is Looking for Trouble

There is not a writer on this planet who doesn't start out with goals that couldn't be described as "lofty." Words like "best-selling," "prize-winning," "critically acclaimed," and my favorites "all-American" and "epic" are tossed around as if one is describing a new Clint Eastwood movie. The reality is, writers would likely be better off if they kept the following words in their vocabulary: focus, reality, discipline, finish, completion, consistency, improvement, patience, and patience (yes, I'm well aware that patience is listed twice). I'm all for goals. I'm all for *big goals*, as becoming a writer requires them, as well as pushing ourselves far beyond our comfort levels—but often writers are doing themselves a huge disservice by setting up goals that are impossible to reach. Writing a memoir is difficult business, so why not take some satisfaction with every step you take? Setting goals that are realistic but still force you to stretch your skills as a writer will keep you on track and will put you in a position of having to improve your craft as well, and you'll be a better writer in the end as a result. So how do you go about setting goals that push you to improve but aren't ultimately setting you up for failure?

- Be realistic. While you may have *The New York Times* best-selling author on your list of things to do before you turn forty, does not reaching that goal actually suggest you're not a successful writer? No. I assure you it does not.

- Celebrate the steps along the way. Finishing a difficult chapter can feel incredibly rewarding, as can getting three comments on a blog post, your first article published, and of course, landing that first book deal. If you only celebrate the major milestones, you'll be facing much disappointment in your writing career.

- Create goals that you can achieve on both smaller and larger time frames. What do you want to do today, this week, this month?

- If you find it helpful to categorize your goals, go for it. I like to have lists for different goals I want to achieve. While writing this book, my main objective was to finish on time! However, I also knew I had to start making plans for promotion. I kept a timeline of which chapters I was going to write when, but also kept other lists of goals. For example, "outline blog post ideas, develop Twitter following, and connect with other writers via social media" were kept on a separate list from "finish chapter seven" and "find writer to interview about writer's groups." Likewise, I have a longer list of those "loftier" goals.

WHY A WRITER WITHOUT A DEADLINE IS LOOKING FOR TROUBLE

Without deadlines writers tend to NEVER STOP WORKING, therefore I think deadlines are pretty important. To quote Chris Baty, creator of National Novel Writing Month (a.k.a. NaNoWriMo) and author of *No Plot? No Problem!* "A deadline is, simply put, optimism in its most ass-kicking form." I have to say I agree with Baty. Without a deadline, prose can always be improved, chapters can forever be tinkered with, and there is always something that can be changed. On the flip side, it's certainly easy enough to get distracted by family, jobs, life, and my best friend, the DVR player. Obviously it's much easier to have a deadline when one is being imposed on you by an agent or a publisher, but barring that option *for now*, how can you keep yourself motivated and on track without a big looming contractual deadline circled in red on your calendar?

Here are a few things to keep in mind when thinking about creating goals and setting a deadline for your work:

- Do I work better under pressure? Or do I like to work in a completely stress-free fashion?
- Do I like to work in short bursts that I can accomplish when I have a short period of time available to me, or do I need a long stretch of time to feel like I'm truly accomplishing something?
- How much time do I reasonably have to work on my memoir? Who will be looking at my memoir when it is finished? Are they willing to look at it at certain stages? Will they look at chapters or do they prefer to look at a full draft? Are they willing to give me a deadline?

While you think a deadline imposed by a writing group member (and more on those shortly) or from a writing class just isn't the same as a deadline from a publisher, think again. Once you, "activate your deadline" to borrow a phrase from Chris Baty, you may be surprised by how reluctant you'll feel to miss it. Most writers feel a deep-seated desire to take their craft seriously, and ultimately don't take deadlines lightly. If you're able to make a commitment to turn in pages to a friend, editor, or instructor, chances are you'll find yourself working extraordinarily hard to honor this commitment.

Create a Writing Schedule

Sometimes keeping yourself on a writing schedule can be made easier by having a visual version of your schedule to refer to. I found it incredibly helpful when working on this book to be able to view my progress and to be able to check off portions of my work that I had completed. It was incredibly satisfying to watch as slowly but surely the items on my schedule were crossed off. I was also able to make some notes about which sections would require some further research, an interview, or perhaps some additional reading. That way I was always prepared as to what each portion of my book had in store for me. I was also able to skip around a little bit. When I was on vacation, I decided to work on one chapter that I knew wouldn't require any reference materials, and would be especially easy for me to write. Here are some of the biggest benefits of creating a writing schedule:

- A schedule helps you visualize how much you have to write and when (how many words per day or per week) in order to reach your goal.
- It helps you feel accomplished by letting you check off tasks you've finished. It's an adult way of giving yourself a big gold star.
- It's a no-denial-no-excuse way of working. If that list isn't shrinking, you know you're not doing the work.
- By adding in notes about sections that might require extra work or research, you'll always be prepared for what each portion of your book is going to throw at you. There are no surprises.

Defining Your Deadlines: A Sample Writing Schedule

DEADLINE:	OBJECTIVE:	WHAT YOU NEED TO GET THERE.
#1 by the end of the week	Flesh out idea for opening of memoir. What I have right now just isn't working.	Reread journal entries. Revisit a couple of memoirs that inspire me, as this section has been troubling me for a long time.

#2 by the end of the month	Decide on structure for book. Have been debating back and forth between two different versions—like them both. Need to make decision by next meeting with writing group.	Opinion of writer's group member after I've had time to mull it over a bit longer.
#3 Daily— to end of the month	Morning pages. I've been doing Natalie Goldberg's "morning pages" from *Writing Down the Bones* and it's been very helpful. Want to continue doing this throughout the month. Exercises in *Writing and Selling Your Memoir*.	Get up half an hour earlier. Might need to go to bed earlier during the week. One hour on Saturday or Sunday afternoons.
#4 in six months	I want to get a first draft of half of my manuscript finished six months from now. I'm envisioning this being about eight chapters or approximately 35,000 words.	I need to focus on writing two chapters per month. I will work one hour every morning before work, and will revise those pages after dinner. Will carve out time on Saturday mornings and Sunday afternoons as well. Will keep regular meetings with writer's group.

When That Deadline Passes You By: The So-Called "I Don't Have Enough Time" Dilemma.

You set a deadline, you fully intended to meet it, but suddenly a month has flown by and all you have to show for yourself are some ill-advised Internet purchases and extraordinarily well-organized closets. I know the feeling, I've been the girl with loads of returns to make and a closet that would impress Martha Stewart herself. So what do you do? I'm a firm believer that when things go wrong, it's time to make a list. Where exactly is that time of yours going? If you can't say with complete certainty "volunteering at the local food pantry" or "raising sextuplets," then it's time to figure out exactly *what it is* you're actually doing. Setting out to write a memoir is going to take nothing short of a major time commitment and discipline from you, so the following exercise should show you once and for all where you can carve out some time to write.

EXERCISE
THE SO-CALLED I DON'T HAVE ENOUGH TIME DILEMMA

Spend a week keeping track of what you do. And when I say "what you do" I mean *everything* you do. The idea here is to search for blocks of time that can be used in a more productive fashion. Yes, you may have to give up a few precious hours of *Jersey Shore* viewing or even sleep in favor of writing, but if it's your dream to write your memoir, and you're under the impression that you don't have enough time to do it, I'm by all means going to do everything in my power to prove that this isn't the case. I've included a handy worksheet so that you can monitor your activities and prove to yourself that there is time to write *somewhere* during your day (or night).

> **QUICK INSPIRATION:** *The tale of how John Grisham wrote his first novel* A Time to Kill *is part of book publishing lore. He wrote the now famous novel over a three-year period in the early morning hours while working an incredibly stressful, 60–80 hour a week job as a lawyer. He also had a wife and two young kids. Proof positive that if you have the desire to write, you will manage to find the time.*

The So-Called I Don't Have Enough Time Dilemma Worksheet

TIME	ACTIVITY	TIME	ACTIVITY
5:00 A.M.		2:30 P.M.	
5:30 A.M.		3:00 P.M.	
6:00 A.M.		3:30 P.M.	
6:30 A.M.		4:00 P.M.	
7:00 A.M.		4:30 P.M.	
7:30 A.M.		5:00 P.M.	
8:00 A.M.		5:30 P.M.	
8:30 A.M.		6:00 P.M.	
9:00 A.M.		6:30 P.M.	
9:30 A.M.		7:00 P.M.	
10:00 A.M.		7:30 P.M.	
10:30 A.M.		8:00 P.M.	
11:00 A.M.		8:30 P.M.	
11:30 A.M.		9:00 P.M.	
12:00 P.M.		9:30 P.M.	
12:30 P.M.		10:00 P.M.	
1:00 P.M.		10:30 P.M.	
1:30 P.M.		11:00 P.M.	
2:00 P.M.		11:30 P.M.	

Find Your Achilles Heel

Take a few minutes to review the list you made on the So-Called I Don't Have Enough Time Dilemma Worksheet. Are you completely satisfied with how you spend your day? Are there some places where you feel like you could improve? We all have our Achilles heels when it comes to writing, and mine is found on Lifetime television everyday starting at 1 p.m. in the form of three consecutive hours of *Grey's Anatomy*. Such a good show! But since knowledge is power, and I was able to alert myself to the black hole where my time was falling every day, I was able to win this particular battle (under no circumstances did I let myself get *near* the television in the afternoon). Believe it or not, it wasn't until I actually made an effort to keep track of where my time was going that I was made completely aware of how much time I was sinking into my new-found medical drama habit. It was quite eye-opening, and thanks to the worksheet, I was able to gain a large chunk of my life back, which I can now devote to more productive projects.

FIVE IDEAS: HOW TO INSERT MORE WRITING TIME INTO YOUR LIFE

- Taking public transportation instead of driving. You can write on the bus or subway, catch up on your memoir reading, or revise your pages.
- Getting up an hour earlier or more every day.
- Cutting out television.
- Writing during your lunch hour at work.
- Say "no" to every other invitation you get to go out and write instead.

You've heard it before, most likely from your mother, when there's a will, there's a way. Is it a cliché? Yes. Are many clichés 100 percent true? Also a yes. If you have a story inside of you that you're determined to write, you're not going to let something like a job, the many demands of family life, your rocking social life, or the season finale of *Lost* (okay, maybe that) get in the way of your story. I know it's hard—writing *is hard—but* with commitment, determination, and of course, that incredibly good story of yours, you'll figure out a way to get there. And oh, the next chapter should help quite a bit, too.

CHAPTER EIGHT:

The Three Major Distractions: How to Avoid Them So You Can Stay Focused and Produce Your Best Work

I t's amazing how many things suddenly need tending to—*urgently and immediately*—the very second you sit down to write. We've already gone over the importance of deadlines, and I hope you've taken that seriously and circled a date on the calendar with a huge red pen. And I know you've just completed the "The So-Called I Don't Have Enough Time Dilemma Worksheet" (see page 127), and you've noticed that you spend two hours a day playing video games or carving miniature animal sculptures out of soap—but if you're anything like me (or most writers for that matter), there is something *painful* about sitting down to actually write, even though you sincerely love doing it. Like most writers, you probably need to "distract-proof" yourself. If any of the following statements ring true to you, you undoubtedly need to read the following section and learn to distract-proof yourself once and for all. The second you sit down to write:

- You realize you can't possibly concentrate if the room you write in is such a mess, and you tidy up first.
- You realize you can't concentrate in such a sterile environment and must inject some life into the room by messing it up a bit first.

- You need to get in touch with your inner Virginia Woolf and can't possibly proceed unless you have a "room of one's own," which is currently impossible since you have a family or roommates, therefore you can't write.
- You *must* pay all of your bills immediately.
- You need to write a letter to an aunt you haven't corresponded with in years.
- You need to look at gift registries of friends who are newly engaged.
- You check out real estate listings.
- You get on Facebook, Twitter, etc.
- You run out to the gym even though you haven't been in eight months (if not now, when?).
- You suddenly feel an overwhelming desire to take up the art of French pastry (or some other unexplored hobby).
- You must write your local congressman about a broken street lamp.

Sound familiar? We've all been there. This past weekend I made a ridiculous amount of homemade granola cereal (and I've already come clean about my *Grey's Anatomy* habit). Writers get distracted. It's part of the process! But you can make a decision right now. Do you want to distract-proof yourself and learn to stay focused? Or do you want to ignore the signs that you're distracted and continue feeling guilty about the lack of work you're producing? It's totally up to you. (Just a hint here, but I recommend choosing the former.) After over a decade of working with all different kinds of authors, I've realized that while there are all kinds of distractions, they tend to fall into three categories. Authors are distracted by their jobs, their family and friends, and perhaps most of all, by themselves. What do I mean by that? Authors can be their own worst enemies, convincing themselves that they don't have the chops to pull off the task at hand, which is a dangerous road to drive down. So how do writers manage to stay on task? By learning to identify and successfully maneuver around what I like to call "the three major distractions."

THE THREE MAJOR DISTRACTIONS

MAJOR DISTRACTION #1:

Your Job: Why You Should Not Quit Under Any Circumstances (Related to the Writing of Your Book Anyway)

One very popular train of thought among writers is this: "I know I could write a really amazing book if I could just quit my job." The writer then usually goes into detail about how he will tell his boss to shove it the second he gets a book deal. Every time I hear this phrase, which is *a lot,* I'm forced to play the role of "the dream crusher." My role as dream crusher generally involves explaining that a) there is no guarantee that your book will even sell, b) advances are lower than ever, and c) if you were lucky to get your first book published, how can you guarantee that you will be able to get a second book deal and continue that stream of income? A friend once put it this way, he thought that getting an agent meant your "career was being sent to you in a FedEx package." Not so. And while a good agent will certainly help you get your memoir in shape and your foot in the door, quitting your job is a premature move. So if you can't quit, how can you make that tricky combination of writing and holding onto that job work? It may help to keep in mind that there are more than just financial reasons for hanging onto that day job. While we'll get into the ins and outs of developing a platform and brand for you as a writer later, let me just say now that by disconnecting yourself from the workforce, you're also disconnecting yourself from quite a bit of opportunity, and that goes beyond the obvious benefit of getting a paycheck. What am I talking about?

Let Your Job Inspire You in Unexpected Ways

Let me ask you this. Would Frank McCourt's memoir *Angela's Ashes* have been as intriguing had he not worked as a public school teacher in New York City? His job history became part of his charm, and rarely do you read an article about Frank McCourt that doesn't mention it; it was even the subject of his third memoir. McCourt's background as a teacher became part of the book's hook. While it ultimately didn't matter at all what McCourt did for a living, the media did catch onto the fact that he was a teacher—they loved his rags-to-riches story. McCourt's background as a teacher made him even more appealing, and this certainly helped in the publicity department, which is never a bad thing in the book world.

Another example is Julie Powell, author of *Julie and Julia*. Would Powell have been inspired to cook every single recipe in *Mastering the Art of French Cooking* and blog about it were she not so utterly bored by her day job?

I think it's possible that many of her readers don't even remember what her day job was; we just know it was pretty dreadful. But what does it matter? Her boredom resulted in a project that really struck a chord and inspired a popular blog, a best-selling book, and a hit film starring Meryl Streep—not to mention a year's worth of marvelous meals. Would she have done all this if she had worked at *Gourmet* magazine? Probably not. Or if she had, it may not have had the same genuine feeling behind it, which is exactly what her readers related to.

That being said, I completely understand how difficult it is to balance family, work, and writing. We spend an inordinate amount of our lives at work. It's challenging to find the time to throw in a load of laundry much less sketch out some ideas for a chapter of your memoir. But I stand by my position that you need to learn to balance your work life with your writing life. While I understand that it's difficult to separate the work life from your creative endeavors, remember that countless writers have managed to balance the two. While it takes extraordinary discipline to add "memoir writing" to a full schedule, the old adage about busy people being more apt to get things done tends to be true. I have worked with writers with all different kinds of work situations—from nine to five jobs, to stay at home moms, to graduate students—and those who were employed full time or had demanding schedules tended to have the most success in meeting a deadline, working productively and consistently, as well as being able to wear all of the hats—marketer, salesperson, self-promoter, etc., that are required of writers today.

Following are a few thoughts for getting through rough patches at work and for getting used to the idea of blending your work life with your creative life.

- Your job, whether it be teacher (think Frank McCourt), secretary (think Julie Powell), or swordfishing boat captain (think Linda Greenlaw), can actually help enhance your profile as a writer.
- Your job brings you into contact with potentially hundreds of people who will buy your book when it's published.
- If you truly dislike your job, use it as inspiration to improve your craft and stretch your creativity.
- Force yourself to take a lunch break and use it to do writing exercises or use your lunch break to read. Staying up to date on the latest memoirs will keep you inspired.
- Start a book group at work. Finding a fellow writer or memoir lover at the office might be helpful.
- Learn to turn off work problems the second you walk through the door. If you have trouble doing this, write about them!

MAJOR DISTRACTION #2:
Your Friends & Family:
The Well-Meaning Time Suckers

I love my family. But I've also had to learn to work around them. Any of you who have young children are especially familiar with this concept. I've had to learn to block out the shrill sound of Elmo's voice and the theme song to Thomas the Train, and I've learned to resist the urge to pick up a large pile of toys before I sit down to work—I just pretend they aren't there. I am also blessed with a group of wonderful friends. But sometimes I just have to say no to drinks or a brunch invitation or leave an E-mail unanswered for a little bit longer than I would normally like. Do I want to be out having cocktails every chance I get? Obviously! Would this book have ever been written if I went out whenever I wanted or let Elmo and his merry band of Muppets get the better of me? Most definitely not. So, how exactly do you manage to get your book written without alienating your loved ones?

Just Say No: The Fine Art of Setting Boundaries

If "write your memoir" is on the top of your list of goals, you need to get used to the simple fact that you might have to miss out on a few things in order to maintain finishing your book as a top priority.

- If going out with friends and colleagues remains a top distraction, dedicate one or two weekends a month (only you can decide how social you really need to be) to socializing. Then make sure that the weekends you devote to writing are just that—devoted to writing.
- If volunteering for child's school functions or socializing for your job is getting in the way for you, ask yourself, "What would happen if I just said no to this next time?" Chances are, absolutely nothing. The world would keep spinning if

someone else brought the vanilla cupcakes or you missed an occasional cocktail hour. Remember, your writing is as important as the kids' Halloween party; it's okay to make your writing a priority from time to time.

- If your friends and family don't understand what it is you are devoting so much time to, explain that it is important to you and you'd appreciate it if they'd respect your decision to devote some of your free time to this pursuit. Some people golf, some play tennis, children play soccer, we all have various activities that take up our time. Why should writing be any different than taking time out to go to the gym? It's a release and it's important. That being said, this is no excuse to play that role of the prima donna writer. Just because you're following your desire to write in earnest does not mean the world needs to fall at your feet.

MAJOR DISTRACTION #3

You: When You Are Your Own Worst Enemy

And now for the third, and quite likely, the largest distraction. That most likely would be *you*, my friend. I know you've dutifully made your So-Called I Don't Have Enough Time Dilemma Worksheet (see page 127), and I hope you've already started setting some boundaries in the name of getting more writing done, but often writers set obstacles for themselves that go beyond your typical time crunch issues. I'm talking about the self-doubt and self-esteem issues that can plague authors and often result from some of the ridiculous myths that are flying around out there about the writing world. Allowing yourself to fall prey to the self-doubt can be incredibly destructive, as can believing some of the utter nonsense that's floating out there on the Internet about the wild world of writing. Developing a thick skin and knowing a little bit more about what it's really like to be a writer can stop you from heading down this destructive path and wasting precious energy feeling badly about yourself when you have absolutely no business doing so. So what the heck am I talking about anyway?

When the Probationary Period Ends

All writers feel energized by new projects. When things are going well with your memoir and you're on a roll, you can actually envision your life as a successful writer. You can probably see yourself signing copies of your book at a local bookstore. You can imagine how it will feel to sign your first contract with the fountain pen you bought when you first realized you really wanted to be a writer. You wake up early every day—not frustrated that you have to wake up early, but energized—this is your time to write! Writing first thing in the morning is the best way to start the day! But then the "probationary period" ends and you begin to feel differently. Maybe you stumbled over a difficult section, and that evil enemy, self-doubt, starts to creep in. Suddenly, getting up at 5:30 is a royal pain in the ass—I mean, it's freezing cold and dark outside, you could be under your warm duvet! What the heck are you doing getting out of bed at that hour to work on your stupid memoir that no one is going to want to read anyway? Sound familiar? Then your probationary period has probably ended. The initial love of the project has worn off, and while I guarantee you'll get it back, you've hit your first major bump and need to be coaxed back into the groove you had going. I warn you, it isn't always easy. But once you realize that writing, like everything else, has its ups and downs (some are much bigger than others), you will learn to ride out these waves and eventually even anticipate them. Does hitting a bottom mean you suck? *No.* Nor does it mean you will never write again or reach your dream of selling your memoir. Does an upswing—one of those periods where everything you write is really great—mean you're so wonderful that you don't need to work as hard? Um, another big no. The key here is pacing, learning to take things in stride, and accepting that no matter how well or how absolutely terribly things are going, you're just as good of a writer as you were yesterday. It's how you handle the situation that makes you a *capable author*. And trust me, being able to handle such situations and carry onto the next stage is what enables some authors to make it through to the other side and not others.

The Myth of the Perfect (or Even Good) First Draft

Do not allow yourself to think for even a single minute that anyone in the history of writing has every produced a decent first draft of anything. If you allow yourself to believe this, you will end up feeling terrible and will end up shopping for shoes online for six weeks instead of writing. It's entirely possible that someone will try to convince you that they've in fact written a decent first draft—and they very well may *believe* they've done so, but this "faux first draft" they are taunting you with would actually be the result of several months if not years of careful planning, organizing, and revising. First drafts are for your eyes only. They are the only way a writer can truly get what is in his head onto paper, see what's there, and then make an intelligent decision as to how to proceed. As I mentioned in chapter six, in her book *Bird by Bird: Some Instructions on Writing and Life*, Anne Lamott has an entire chapter devoted to the topic of what she calls "Shitty First Drafts." She describes them as follows:

> The first draft is the child's draft, where you let it all pour out and then let it romp all over the place, knowing that no one is going to see it and that you can shape it later. You just let this childlike part of you channel whatever voices and visions come through and onto the page. If one of the characters wants to say, "Well, so what, Mr. Poopy Pants?," you let her. No one is going to see it. If the kid wants to get into really

sentimental, weepy, emotional territory, you let him. Just get it down on paper, because there may be something great in those six crazy pages that you would never have gotten to by more rational, grown-up means. There may be something in the very last line of the very last paragraph on page six that you just love, that is so beautiful or wild that you now know what you're supposed to be writing about, more or less, or in what direction you might go—but there was no way to get to this without first getting through the first five and a half pages.

In other words, the first draft is all about letting your "freak flag fly". Go crazy, experiment, try every possible combination of words and scenarios. And know that when you read them back to yourself for the first time that they might not sound so great— but that's the point. It isn't a sign that you should give up. Please resist every urge to throw your manuscript out the window. This is the process! You take a deep breath, put the pages away, get up the next morning and you begin again.

The Myth That the Writer's Life Is a Glamorous One

It is entirely possible that, at some point during the writing of your memoir, you will stop what you're doing mid-sentence, take a look at your surroundings, and wonder "where is my oak-paneled library with the built-in, floor-to-ceiling bookshelves?" I myself have wondered this on several occasions. You may also be collecting your mail one afternoon and feel puzzled that there are only bills and no exclusive invitations to cocktail parties with Jonathan Franzen, Candace Bushnell, and various *New Yorker* staff writers. You may begin to feel slightly depressed and that your life is lacking on some level. This is totally understandable and not your fault in any way. Hollywood, television, and the media in general have led writers to believe that by simply putting pen to paper, life is to change drastically and in the most exciting of ways. Dry martini you ask? Coming right up! Right after I deliver this glass of champagne to Mr. Rushdie who is holding court with the ghosts of Dorothy Parker and Philip Roth. I would like to dispel this myth and let you know that there is little to no reality to it. Why am I insistent on playing the role of dream crusher once again? Because on too many occasions I have heard authors complain that they can't get ahead because they a) don't have the right connections, b) don't have a way to break into the business, or c) don't have a proper space to write (the "room of one's own issue"). Don't let yourself think for a second that just because you're a homemaker from Oshkosh, Wisconsin, writing in your daughter's bedroom while she's away at college, that you don't stand a chance at becoming a successful author. Yes, working at a magazine or newspaper certainly makes breaking into the business easier, but if you read the author bios of some of the writers you enjoy, you will see that a good many of them were not born in New York City, did not write regularly for magazines, and were not on staff at newspapers before becoming published authors. Many authors started with smaller steps and built their careers piece by piece. This means they had to go through the process of creating a platform, writing a book, and seeking out the right agent (and more on that soon I swear). Nearly every author has had to make the connections. It's possible to do, and not being a part of the so-called literary elite is no excuse for not being able to break into the business.

I agree with a certain Virginia Woolf that we need a "room of one's own"—and I can tell you that I'm still waiting for mine. Not having a room of one's own is another popular reason that writers are not able to complete their work, and I'm here to tell you that if you show me a writer who truly believes this is the reason she can't write, I'm absolutely certain I could buy her a castle and she'd find a completely different reason to not finish her memoir. We've already gone over the major distractions in this chapter, and many writers convince themselves that they "just need their own space" and, if they had it, all of their problems would magically be solved. If you are serious about writing, know that a corner will truly do if that's what you have to work with. I have a section in my apartment that's devoted to storing all of my materials for writing this book (hey, it's New York, we don't have a lot of space), and I write at the kitchen table. Having a section devoted to this project keeps me organized, but more importantly, it signifies that this project is important.

> **QUICK TIP:** *If you find yourself repeatedly getting distracted, start to pay attention and see if there's a pattern to be found. After a couple of particularly nonproductive weeks, I suddenly had a couple of days where the words were flying freely. What was the difference? I had left the house before I started writing. This made a big difference for me in the productivity department so I'm always sure to get out for a walk, go out for a cup of coffee, or I simply run a few errands before I start working. For me, starting the process with some interaction with the outside world seems to result in a more productive day. Learn what works for you.*

Believe me, I realize there are times when you need to escape, and barring the availability of an entire room in your house, or a nook that's quiet enough, consider the following options. They may not be quite what Virginia had in mind, but hey, throw a good latte or a cupcake into the mix and I dare say the local coffee shop starts to look way better than that solitary room.

- cooperative writer's spaces (these quiet spaces that you can rent quarterly for a relatively low amount of money are becoming more popular and are definitely cheaper than office space)

- your local coffee shop
- the neighborhood diner
- a park bench on a nice day
- the local branch of your public library (they often have free Wi-Fi as well)
- university libraries or private, membership-only libraries

CHAPTER NINE:

Being Stuck Productively

I firmly believe that part of being a good writer is knowing when to stop yourself from working and take a proper break. All writers experience periods of time when what they're working on simply isn't working—sentences don't gel, your ideas seem ridiculous, and it takes hours to get anything at all accomplished. Of course we all experience those mini-periods when we feel stuck, have to rewrite something a few times, or feel unsure about an idea and have to start a section over, but what I'm talking about here is Stuck with a capital "S." Nothing works. You feel totally uninspired. You're wondering why you ever thought you could write to begin with and are on the verge of giving up completely. You start to have thoughts along the lines of "Hey, maybe I should take up fencing or bird-watching." You'll do anything to avoid your computer. Your spouse innocently asking, "How's your book coming along?" is grounds for immediate divorce. We've all been there, and it can be awful. But being stuck is simply part of the process. We simply can't be 100 percent productive all of the time, as much as we'd like that to be the case. The way I see it, when it comes to being Stuck (with the capital "S" variety), you have a choice to make. Do you want to be stuck productively or unproductively?

The unproductive way to be stuck includes spending entire hours or days relentlessly trying to work on a single sentence, obsessing over the fact that you've wasted an entire day working on a single sentence, and lastly, being utterly miserable about your lack of productivity. Sound familiar? Is this how you really want to spend precious writing time? On the flip side, being a writer requires so much more than actually writing, you can use this "stuck" time to do a number of things that will make you a more informed, well-rounded, and lastly, well-rested and more productive writer.

GET BACK TO THE BUSINESS OF BEING A WRITER

If you have the discipline to recognize that you are truly Stuck, and your brain genuinely needs a break, then this is the perfect opportunity to accomplish many things that tend to linger on a writer's ever growing to-do list. When I find I just can't do any more writing, I'll take some time to deal with the "business of being a writer."

This might mean coming up with some blog post ideas, searching for blogs that have audiences that might be interested in my topic, looking for new people to follow on Twitter, or looking for books to read for inspiration. Maybe I'll pick up a memoir I've been meaning to read, as that usually gets me back on track very quickly.

While I could berate myself for "not writing," that would fall into the category of "unproductive stuck," and if I've just posted five comments on blogs, noted three that might be potential markets for my book, gained two followers on Twitter, and started reading a fantastic memoir that has gotten me excited about my project again, how is that not working?

Ten Valuable Things You Can Do When You're Stuck:

- keep up-to-date by reading a memoir
- read some industry websites
- work on your vocabulary
- start a blog or stockpile blog posts if you already have a blog
- make a list of blogs you like that pertain to your subject matter
- research writer's conferences
- meet a local bookseller
- work on your Twitter presence
- make a list of publications you'd like to submit your work to
- find a mentor

REALITY CHECK: *If you are finding yourself Stuck every couple of weeks, it's highly possible that you are using "writer's block" as an excuse to avoid writing and you're not really all that stuck. While we all run out of steam from time to time, it's not reasonable to take a break every couple of weeks. If you find yourself doing this, take an honest look at what's keeping you from actually tending to your writing.*

Be Inspired by a Good Book

We talked about the importance of keeping up to date on the latest and most successful memoirs in chapter one, and how being familiar with other books in your genre is crucial to your success as a writer. Being Stuck is the perfect time to dive into a book, whether it be a memoir you haven't read but have been anxious to dip into, or a novel you've been curious about. Nothing encourages a writer to get back to the act of writing than reading a good book. Let other people inspire you with their thoughts on structure, language, style, voice, etc. Sit back and enjoy the end result of a book without having to think about how you're responsible for every single word of the story.

One Really *Is* the Loneliest Number: The Writer Burn-Out

There is a reason Harry Nilsson's hit song "One" has been covered by everyone from Three Dog Night to Aimee Mann. One *is* the loneliest number. Writing a memoir, sitting alone for hours at your desk, dealing with memories, some of which may be painful, is undeniably a lonely endeavor. I have found in my work with memoirists that this sort of work is particularly draining, and it is essential that the writer develop a good support system. It's entirely possible that your feeling Stuck is the result of feeling burned-out, and you just might need to get away from your material for a while before you decide to stick your manuscript in the drawer and forget about your book altogether. Stephen King talks about the need for a good support system in his memoir *On Writing* (King is referring to fiction here, but no matter, his advice applies to all writers universally). King writes about the time in his life when he wrote *Carrie* as especially grim. He was teaching, struggling to be a writer, and Friday would roll around and he would feel like "he'd spent the week with jumper cables clamped to my brain." He credits his wife Tabby with getting him through intact. If you've been working too hard, sifting through memories, working on your memoir all hours of the night and are feeling like you've hit a wall, know it's okay to put it aside for a while. Make time to hang out with friends and family if you've been too focused on your book. Besides, we wouldn't have memoirs to write if we didn't have memories, right? So go out and make some memories. Your book will be waiting for you when you get back.

And If Nothing Else Works, Listen to Luca Spaghetti

Elizabeth Gilbert had to go all the way to Italy to learn to learn how to do nothing. Unable to fully relax and enjoy her Italian vacation dedicated solely to *pleasure* (typical American!), her friend Luca Spaghetti suggests she master the art of "il bel far niente," the beauty of doing nothing. It's not unusual for authors to find that they can clearly see what they need to do with their work and how they need to do it only once they've stepped away from it. And while any writer will tell you that discipline is a key component to success, it is equally important to recognize when a break is needed. After over a decade of working with authors, I have seen how essential it can be to put the writing away (temporarily). Don't be afraid of admitting to yourself that you might need to tune out for a short while. Watch a movie, walk in the park, go shopping—do whatever you need to do to clear your head. It's not admitting defeat; it's about getting the distance you need to get yourself productive and working as soon as possible. Feeling guilty while being away from your memoir just isn't helpful (that's what I'm taking from Mr. Spaghetti anyway).

CHAPTER TEN:

Editing Your Work and Improving Your Craft

You have a draft of a manuscript, or at least a few decent chapters, so you can get on the phone and start calling agents right? Then you can just stick a few copies of your work in the mail, and kick back and watch the latest season of the *Jersey Shore* or maybe the BBC version of *Pride and Prejudice* if that's more your style, right? The answers are a big NO and NO. I know what you're thinking: You've worked incredibly hard on perfecting your voice, you've managed to find an absolutely fantastic hook, your structure is working great, and you don't want to waste another second sitting around when you could be getting an agent, letting them polish your work and landing you a massive six-figure multibook deal. And then there's the cherry on the sundae that's the movie deal right? If you read some of the industry websites, it can appear that this happens quite often, but let me assure you that a) for every writer who gets a massive first book deal, there are countless others who get a modest first book deal or no deal at all and b) you have absolutely no idea how hard that author worked to get that first book deal. There may very well have been years (yes, I said years) of revisions, rejections, and complete rewrites before a first offer was made. So, please don't think that pressing "print" on the computer means that you're ready to start submitting your work to agents or editors. Does that mean you won't be ready to do so in the near future? Of course not. This chapter is all about preparation and how to determine when you're actually ready to make that big step that is showing your work to a professional.

THE PREMATURE SUBMISSION: JUST DON'T DO IT

The one major mistake nearly every author makes is sending out her materials far too soon. I understand completely that writers have worked hard, and are anxious for feedback, and are even more anxious for a jumpstart on their careers. But let me tell you right now that a literary agent is *not* the first person who should be giving you feedback on your work. Nor should they be the second or the third. Your work should not land on the desk of an industry professional until you've dedicated a serious amount of time to revising, studying your craft, editing, proofreading, letting your work simmer a little bit, and then revising once again. Do I think you need to wait a year or even six months between the time you print out your full draft and you send out that first query letter? Not necessarily. But do remember how hard you've worked. You don't want to blow your chances by sending out work that's just not ready. Agents see countless submissions from unknown authors every day, but here's the thing, all it really takes is a well written query and some well crafted pages to pique our interest. Why? A well prepared submission package with polished pages is truly that rare.

Don't Be an Almost

I've had many "almosts" land on my desk. What's an "almost?" An "almost" is a writer with a great idea, but it needs to be tweaked because the execution is off. Or maybe the idea is truly there, but the writing is really rough and you can't tell if the author needs editing or just can't write. Perhaps the writing is really strong for a few pages, but then it all just falls apart, which can be such a disappointment for an agent! I know what you're thinking: "Hey, isn't it your job to sit around your big office with red pencils and tell the guy how to fix all that stuff?" Well, yes and no. A good agent will help you develop your work and get it ready for submission, but seriously, we don't have all the time in the world. If you're "almost" ready for representation, we're just not going to be interested. I need to be able to tell with complete confidence that a potential client has the ability and willingness to pull of the project they are proposing. I'm not going to invest my valuable time editing a manuscript to find out, "Oops, I guess this woman actually can't write that well. She needs some classes!" Giving guidance, editing, and direction is one thing. Not being able to tell exactly what an author needs and not being clear as to what an author is capable of is entirely another.

So, do you want to be an "almost" or one of those rare writers who cause agents to stop what they're doing and get you on the phone to find out if you've found an agent already? If you've chosen the latter, which I hope you have, then I suggest you take the time get yourself some really good feedback on your work.

Getting Feedback: Why It's Essential to Find a Good Reader

You've worked hard to get your memoir to where it is. But how do you know it's the best it can be? Where can you get some feedback? And here's a puzzle: How do you know if that the feedback is any good? The good news is that there are many options for getting feedback today, and I'm not talking about your friends and family (who are not the most reliable sources, by the way). I'm talking about places to get unbiased, helpful criticism that you can use to improve your work before you even think about sending it to agents. Here are some of the many benefits of getting some feedback on your work:

- Good feedback can help you see flaws in your work that you simply aren't able to see yourself.
- A good reader can help you detect patterns, whether good or bad, that may have otherwise gone undetected. You can use reader criticism to correct or expand on these patterns and improve your work.
- Prose is often improved with the help of a good reader.
- An objective reader can be essential in helping out with pacing. If your work is too long or too slow, they're going to pick up on that immediately.
- Polishing your work will make the process of getting an agent easier. A good solid query letter with well edited pages is truly rare!

FIND A VENUE THAT WORKS FOR YOU: WRITERS' GROUPS AND WRITING CLASSES

Writers' Groups

If you're a writer who is passionate about the written word, loves writing more than food and air, and reading is just about your favorite thing to do in the entire world, then trust me, there's a really good chance that there are others nearby who feel exactly the same way that you do. If you haven't seen signs of an already established writers' group in your area (there may be signs for one at a local coffee shop or bookstore), consider starting one. A writers' group, if run properly, can be an incredibly effective way to receive feedback on your work while also honing your skills as an editor. Why bother with your editing skills you ask? Because the better you are at editing, the better you'll be at recognizing areas you need to improve in your own work. Your work will become cleaner and more organized; you'll be in a better position to recognize both your strengths and weaknesses as a writer. Who wouldn't want to be able to do that? I had to work in book publishing for fifteen years to be able to do that!

Are Writers' Groups Right for You?

THE PROS:

- Writers' groups are completely free.
- A group setting can be a great way to socialize and make friends while getting feedback on your work.
- You can hone your editing skills in the process.
- Writer's groups can be a great place to form long-term relationships with writing partners. Some groups stick together for years.

THE CONS:

- If there are not firm ground rules, the group get off track or out of control.
- You have to make sure the criticism you get is in fact helpful.
- It sometimes takes discipline to keep a group going.

> **QUICK TIP:** *Does your writers' group tend to consist of more socializing than work? If your group is headed in that direction, take a cue from this exercise from Natalie Goldberg's book* Old Friend From Far Away: The Practice of Writing Memoir. *She recommends* **no** *conversation whatsoever until each member has completed two twenty-minute writing sessions. After each session is complete, you can read what you've written to each other. The topics are up to you! After you've completed the exercise, it's back to the conversation, coffee, or if you're like me, wine and cocktails.*

Writing Classes

More formal writing classes are an obvious venue for improving your work. The continuing education departments at many universities offer some fantastic classes, and sometimes provide an opportunity to work with professors who teach the university's regular for-credit courses. Online courses are another option. Writer's Digest University (writersdigestuniversity.com) offers some very exciting online programs that will provide you with great tips and actual feedback. The social aspect of a writing class is another added benefit for some, as the classroom environment provides an additional opportunity for networking and making connections.

Are Writing Classes Right for You?

THE PROS:

- You don't necessarily have to read the work of your fellow students, but keep in mind that this depends on how the class is run, as it is important to learn to be critical.
- It's nice to have an actual teacher running the class, providing guidance, feedback, and moderating the discussions that do involve critiquing other students' work.
- Classes provide automatic structure. You are required to be at a certain place at a certain time. This forces you to stay on a particular schedule with your work.
- You can feel confident (if you've carefully selected the class and are comfortable with it) that the criticism from your teacher is coming from someone who is qualified to give it.

THE CONS:

- Classes cost money.
- Classes *do* require you to be at a certain place at a certain time. The bottom line is that this doesn't work for everyone. It's all about what works *for you*.

FINDING A MENTOR

While writers tend to be busy people, almost any writer will tell you that there was someone involved in their career at some point who played a crucial role in getting them to where they are today. That person may have been an editor, a teacher, or a fellow writer with more experience who was willing to offer advice and support. And while you don't want to jump the gun and ask just anyone to be your mentor, I would recommend keeping your eyes open to those in your life who may have something to offer you. Who do you know that may be willing to offer encouragement and open doors? If you do have someone in mind, please make sure that if he is in fact open to mentoring you, that you are respectful of his time as well as his opinions. You can't send him pages and then e-mail him five minutes later if you don't get a response. You also have to choose someone whose opinions you respect. Don't enter a mentor-type relationship if you're going to be contentious every time your mentor offers you criticism. If that's the way you're likely to react to this kind of arrangement, then one-on-one mentoring might not be a good fit for you.

MAKING AND TAKING CRITICISM: THE RIGHT WAY

Writing on your own and reading your work back to yourself is all well and good, but there comes a point when a writer simply has to let go and let someone else actually read his work. It's terrifying, I know. The first time I wrote something and shared it with another person I felt sick to my stomach. What if they thought it was terrible? What if they thought I was a total joke of a writer? How would I ever face them again? But surely they'd lie to me and just tell me it was good to save me the humiliation right? As scary as it is to share your work with an actual human being, it's necessary to take that next step as a writer if you want your writing to improve. If you don't learn to share your work, evaluate and be rational about the criticism you receive, figure out how to incorporate suggestions into your work, and eventually master the fine art of self-editing, your work will stall.

Use the Secrets of a
New York City Book Editor

When you need to offer criticism to another writer, keep the following in mind. I have found that a good editor can get a writer to do almost anything. That being said, all it takes is one off-the-cuff comment to turn your average writer into a giant puddle of panic. How does a good editor do it? A well-written editorial letter will clearly explain an editor's concerns about a project and will by no means let an author think that a particular work is close to being finished or without issue. However, that very same letter will also be sure to point out where the author does something *just right*. The editor will use just the right tone to coax the author into seeing her own strengths, and how she actually has the keys to solving the book's problems right there in her very own manuscript. So how can you use the secrets of a New York City editor to become a positive force in your writer's group or writing class? Here are a few pointers:

- Be the voice of calm. Remember, this is an evaluation, not a debate. Do not argue, raise your voice, or become emotional. This works in two ways: It shows that you are a rational and clear-thinking individual, and it also avoids hurt feelings.

- Avoid starting your comments with statements such as "I didn't like this," "I didn't get this," "I guess this isn't my cup of tea," or "I don't understand INSERT TOPIC HERE." That's a cop-out. There is always something to comment on: structure, voice, pacing, etc. Say something, or you are doing your fellow writer a disservice.

- Whenever possible, use examples of what the writer did right as examples. For instance, "I love how you started chapter three. That was so interesting! I couldn't help but wonder if there was a way to weave that concept into more of the manuscript?"

- Always remember that you are making suggestions and not demands.
- Be careful with your delivery. People do need honest criticism, but remember that you are giving this criticism publicly. How would you feel if you were in their position? If a colleague's first one hundred pages are dreadfully boring, I caution you against saying, "Jim, I've got to be honest with you, I just couldn't get into your memoir until page 120 or so." OUCH. Consider the equally effective, but less awkward, "You know, some really exciting stuff starts happening around chapter six, it's so vivid! Is there anyway you could cut some of the preliminary material and start the story with your trip to Japan?" Get fellow writers thinking and excited about your suggestions—don't put them on the defensive.
- Consider setting criticism guidelines for your group. If you discuss how you feel it is appropriate to give criticism, it can save a lot of problems, hurt feelings, and wasted energy down the line.

Criticism: What to Do With It?

I hope you've managed to give your fellow writers criticism in a way that helps them improve their manuscripts and has created positive energy all around your writers' group. In other words, nothing you've said has resulted in fisticuffs. But eventually, the tables will turn and it will be your turn to sit in the hot seat. How do you handle it when it's your work that's under fire? How can you be sure to get the most out of what your colleagues have to say? Are you supposed to take everything they say as final? What if their comments contradict one another? What if you have really strong feelings about something they say? What if someone in your group is just totally out there? Trusting other people and their opinions about your writing can be scary, and it can take time to develop the kind of relationship where you can feel comfortable simply digesting what your group has to say and incorporating their comments. Following are a few things to keep in mind when it's your work that's under the microscope:

- If you're wondering about the quality of a particular person's assessment, think about how much you agreed or didn't agree with their opinions of other members' work. Did you feel it was on target? Was their criticism helpful?
- Remember that criticism is meant to help get your work to the next level. No one's work is ever perfect the first go around. This is part of the process.
- If two sets of comments are contradictory, it's okay to take sides. It's natural to feel inclined to trust one person's opinion more than another's. That being said, take caution if you are constantly feeling the urge to ignore critical comments, because you are doing yourself a disservice in the process. It's fine to prefer one direction over another, but pay attention. Are you constantly avoiding criticism?
- Feel free to ask questions. Ask for further explanation, but don't be defensive.
- Don't react. Take time to sit with the information you've collected. Digest it, then decide what you want to incorporate.

REALITY CHECK: *Are you rejecting every comment every member of your writers' group or class has to offer? Do you feel that your teacher doesn't know what she's doing? If that's the case, there's a good chance that you are simply refusing to acknowledge that your work can stand to be improved. By refusing to listen to your colleagues, you are putting yourself at risk. Do you think you're really above improvement? Think again. Chances are your work would benefit from revision just like everyone else's.*

A Word on Freelance Editors

I'm often asked by writers if it's helpful to seek out the services of freelance editors. When I receive query letters where an author tells me he's had his manuscript edited by "editor so and so," that particular bit of information is completely irrelevant to me. Is it possible that the work they did with that editor made a big difference? Absolutely! But in my mind, what matters is the final product. If the pages are absorbing, well written, and something that's going to tear me away from whatever else it is I'm doing, I'll read them. It doesn't matter if an outside editor was involved or not. What I'm saying, is having the personal stamp of a professional editor isn't what makes the difference—it's the work itself. If you feel you could use the extra help, and have exhausted your immediate resources, such as your writers' group, local classes, etc., there is nothing wrong with seeking out the services of an outside editor. Just be aware that the act of doing so is not enough to make your work appeal to an agent or an in-house editor.

Take Your Revision Period Seriously

I can't tell you how many times I've gone over major editorial revisions with a client only to have them tell me they'll have them back to me in a week. Really? A week? I suspect they think this is exactly what an agent wants to hear, that there will be a fast turnaround. But truthfully, unless the revisions are incredibly minor, or we're just talking about some light line editing, we know very well that thoughtful, careful editing and writing cannot take place over the course of one week. And sure enough, when I get that e-mail with the attachment a week later, and the manuscript still needs loads of work, I'm not surprised (but I'll admit to now being slightly angry as well). Writing as you know by now requires energy, planning, care, and even time to backtrack and start over again. No matter what you do, it's a process that can't be rushed. While I'm certainly not suggesting you dedicate the next decade to the writing of your memoir, I am saying that you should be reasonable about setting up a time frame in which you can carefully and comfortably work. While I do think that setting a deadline for yourself is essential, you're eliminating any helpful aspects of having a deadline by creating one you have no chance of meeting. Take your revision period seriously. Editing and revising are as important as the initial writing process. After all, there wouldn't be a single decent book to read if no one did this! While this part of the game can be grueling, keep in mind that it's getting you one step closer to where you want to be—having a finished book.

RECOMMENDED READING

BOOKS TO HELP YOU IMPROVE YOUR WORK

Bird by Bird: Some Instructions on Writing and Life by Anne Lamott

If You Want to Write: A Book About Art, Independence and Spirit by Brenda Ueland

On Writing by Stephen King

Old Friend From Far Away: The Practice of Writing Memoir by Natalie Goldberg

On Writing Well by William Zinsser

CHAPTER ELEVEN:

"What's Your Platform?": The Most Common Question a Writer Will Be Asked and How to Answer

"**W**hat's her platform?" I always knew the question was going to come up eventually. I could have submitted the cleanest, most polished manuscript with *The New York Times* bestseller written all over it and the inevitable and often dreaded question of "platform" would still come up. Who is this author and why should we publish her book? Even if it is one of the best we've ever read on the subject and the entire publishing house is smitten? Why will the media care about her? What's so special about this author that the *Today Show* or *Good Morning America* are going to want to book her, and dare we even mention the *O* word? How do we know that we're going to get any return on our investment with this writer?

Are you starting to see why I sometimes dread the platform question? Talent doesn't always come with platform, but unfortunately publishers prefer a package deal. There's quite a few talented people out there, but it takes a unique individual to realize that these days you just can't sit back, mix yourself a martini, toss a fresh piece of paper in a vintage typewriter, and think your words are going to magically find an audience. Publishing books is a business, and publishers want to work with authors who understand this. Talent is obviously required to make a great book, but unfortunately, it doesn't actually help move books out of the local bookstore. This is where platform comes in.

BE THE TOTAL PACKAGE

I can't tell you how many times clients have asked me "So what do publishers want anyway? Good thrillers? Celebrity bios? Vampire stories?" The answer is, they want "the total package." Publishers want a talented author who can produce excellent material, who recognizes that publishing books is in fact *a business* that takes continual and focused efforts, and who has a strong and relevant platform that will help her move their product (yes, books are in fact a product as well as a work of literature). The sooner you realize you need to work as hard at selling your book as you do writing it, the easier this process will be and the more success you'll have as a writer. And here's the secret: The more successful your books are, the more likely it is you'll get a second deal (with more support from that in-house publicity team during the second go-round). While smart authors never rest when it comes to publicity, those who are doing their jobs right find that their efforts are eventually rewarded by some great in-house support. But the bottom line is it's usually never enough, so plan on working hard on pushing yourself and your books for as long as you intend to keep writing them. You put a tremendous amount of effort into writing and creating your work, so why would you simply pass it off to someone else to promote and sell without taking an active role? Don't abandon your book now!

Why You Need to Start Working on Your Platform Now. Literally, Now. Go!

It is never too soon to start developing a platform for your book. If you're thinking "How do you develop a platform when you don't have a book first?", please know that I've heard that question hundreds of times. Great writing careers are simply not born *from books*, but sprung from well-developed, unique, and successful platforms, which by no means need to include a book to get started. Platforms can start on an incredibly small level and increase over time, but know they can't be created overnight—or in a week, or even in a month. Waiting until your agent is ready to send your book out the door is simply too late—and don't even think about waiting until after your book is published. Do you want to compete with another writer who has equally polished material but also has written a column for his local paper for a year that resulted in his getting quoted in *The Miami Herald* regularly, which then led to the publication of an op-ed piece, which resulted in several pieces being published on *The Huffington Post*, who now has a blog with a wide following and teaches seminars? Who do you think a publisher is going to feel has a greater chance of selling books?

Your platform must be systematically created by targeting your audience, developing a following, developing trust with that following, and learning to maintain a relationship with that following. Simply devoting a small amount of time each week to your platform can result in a big payoff down the line. Doing a lot of work now to create a built-in audience means you'll be doing more "maintenance" work in the future rather than scrambling to find readers. There is nothing worse than feeling desperate to get your numbers up when your sales are low—or worse yet, not being able to get a book deal at all because you can't convince a publisher that your talent is guaranteed to come with a built-in audience.

So what exactly is a platform? What should your platform as a memoir writer be sure to include? Basically, a platform is your following as a writer—the built-in audience of readers that come along with you wherever it is you may happen to take them. Many different components can comprise a solid platform, and some writers may excel at some of these and be lacking in others. For example, it's okay if you have a blog that's read by 300,000 people per month for instance, but you don't happen to have much television experience. Every writer is different and the areas of your platform you should focus on really depend on what your expertise is and what makes sense for your particular book topic. A good solid platform can include any combination of the following elements:

- articles or essays you've written
- publications you've worked for
- places you've been quoted
- books you've written
- studies you've conducted
- boards you serve on
- publications where you've been interviewed
- university affiliations
- public speaking you do
- seminars you teach
- the blog or website you maintain (if it has a wide enough readership)

The Anti-Platform Building List: What Not to Do or Say—EVER

On the flip side, there are a few things that a potential agent or publisher just doesn't want to hear about. While these things might in fact be the seeds of a good platform, keep in mind that agents and editors just don't want to hear about seeds. They want to know about platforms that are active; they want to know about audiences that are in plain sight. So please take caution that you don't say any of the following:

- "I plan to start a blog." or "I just started a blog."
- "I'm going to start teaching seminars or classes."

- "I will pitch local papers."
- "I want to write for national magazines."
- "I will hire a publicist."
- "I will create a national media tour."
- "I will read at local bookstores."
- "I will develop relationships with local booksellers."
- "My family, friends, and book club think this is a great idea."
- "I'd love to go on a book tour."
- Or my personal favorite (and any agent will tell you they cringe when they here this one): "I'm happy to go on *Oprah* or other national TV shows."

These all seem like reasonable things to do right? So then what's the problem? The problem is that all of these ideas are passive, not active. Sure, it's great that *you want* to write for national magazines. Who doesn't? But what do we know about this writer? What are the odds that she'll actually be able to get an essay published in *Vogue* or an article published in *Marie Claire*? It's an incredibly competitive environment, and it's competitive for the writers who have already been successfully writing magazine and newspaper articles for years. Then there's the added complication of "lead time." It takes quite a few months for those glossy magazines to be put together, so if your proposal is ready to go, it's going to be a challenge to get an article published in a big glossy publication before sending your memoir out to publishers. And as for Oprah? That's fantastic that you're willing to go on her show (FYI, I'm rolling my eyes here), but please know that every single publisher, agent, and writer in the entire industry has an Oprah fantasy. Yes, we'd all like our clients to be invited to sit on that particular couch. But our wanting it doesn't mean it's going to happen, so please spare yourself the embarrassment of pointing out that you think Oprah would enjoy your book. I will say right now that I truly hope that you are The One—I really do—but please, if you don't learn anything else from this book don't say *that* in a query letter. Promise me, okay?

As for a few of those other items on the list that also seem totally reasonable—and on some level are—let me take a few moments to explain why they are not reasonable ways to go about establishing a platform.

Hiring a Publicist

I've known writers who have worked closely with publicists and have had great results, but these have been writers who have already had a platform, and therefore, the publicist had something to grab onto and expand upon. What I'm getting at here is the idea of having a platform before you even throw your proposal into the ring. What I want you to understand is that hearing the words, "I'll hire a publicist," does not bring on the collective sigh or relief that you would think it does at the editorial meeting at a publisher's office. In fact, it makes no impact at all. It does nothing to couch the fact that this writer in question currently has no platform. So please understand before you write out a big fat check to a publicist that if you haven't done the work of building a platform, publishers are not going to see your willingness to hire one as a reasonable excuse as to why you don't have a built-in audience in place.

The Myth of the Local Bookstore Reading and the Illusive Book Tour

It's difficult to tell authors they've been rejected, but it's also surprisingly heartbreaking to break the news that bookstore readings won't land them on the best-seller list—and furthermore, that there's little chance their publisher is going to send them on a no-expense-spared, whirlwind book tour. Sure, readings make the author feel great; they might sell as many as twenty books to their friends, and a lovely time is had by all sipping chardonnay at the local wine bar afterwards. But does this event ultimately have a huge impact on sales? No. Unless you are on the level of someone like David Sedaris who brings out literally hundreds of people to an event, this just isn't a cost-effective way to sell books. So while yes, by all means set up a few readings in your town to create awareness when your book comes out, meet the booksellers, and create good will, just do not make the mistake of thinking that this is truly platform-building work—it's one part of platform-building work. It's relationship building, self-esteem building, yes, but it's not going to get you on the best-seller list. This brings me to the book tour question. I get this a lot: "How many cities will my book tour include?" Well, generally, I'm afraid the answer is usually zero. Publishers just don't have the funds to invest in tours these days, and authors are rarely sent on tours. Yes, some authors are sent to a few cities, but keep in mind that this is usually because their publicist has managed to get them some media bookings—local television, or maybe if they are very lucky, a national show. If it makes sense, there will be some other appearances, including a bookstore—but as you now know from what you've just read, you're not going to tour the country based on your wonderful ability to read aloud from your book. So again, please don't be disappointed if your publisher isn't sending you on a five-city book tour.

HOW TO BUILD AN INTUITIVE PLATFORM

Now that I've dashed all of your hopes and dreams and have told you that your plans are totally improbable, you might be thinking this is a hopeless endeavor and you should have just bought that book on woodworking or knitting like you were originally thinking. Fear not! I'm going to show you how it is completely in your power to create a platform that will impress agents and editors and will help you build your writing career step by step without feeling like you've taken on a second job. Doesn't that sound better?

While the idea of starting a platform from scratch can sound incredibly intimidating, many memoir writers find that they have more to bring to the platform table than they initially realized. Writing about your personal experience means you may automatically have a leg up on other writers in the platform department. If you take a moment to think back on chapter two where we discussed categories and themes at length, you'll remember that we broke our topics down into various areas of interest. Christina Katz, who wrote the wonderful book *Get Known Before the Book Deal: Use Your Personal Strengths to Grow an Author Platform* wisely insists that platforms be three things: "authentic, organic, and sustainable." Your platform needs to be sincere, flow naturally from your area of expertise and interest, and you need to feel confident you can maintain this platform over an extended period of time. So, start by asking yourself these three platform launch questions:

1. What do I know?
2. Who do I know?
3. What can I do?

What Do I Know?

Well, probably a lot. But what I'm getting at here is what is your area of expertise? You've just mapped out an entire book! It has a theme and, furthermore, a hook. Did you even think that when you were sorting out that hook of yours in chapter two that it would prove to be so incredibly handy when promoting yourself later on? Your hook actually provides all sorts of clues about your area of expertise. And why is this important? Your area of expertise can lead you to many places where a built-in audience for your book is ready and waiting.

> **QUICK TIP:** *If you're struggling with the "I'm not an expert" syndrome, remind yourself, you ARE an expert! You just wrote an entire book on the topic at hand after all! Also remember that the literary world is a place that values quirks, eccentricities, and even downright weirdness. If these words describe you, think about whether you can use these qualities to successfully "brand yourself." Think Malcolm Gladwell and his big hair. Or Stephen King and his Coke bottle glasses.*

Your Master List

My client Melissa Houtte wrote *Alligators, Old Mink & New Money* with her sister Alison. It's a memoir about selling vintage clothes in Brooklyn. Alison and Melissa know a lot about vintage clothes. But when establishing a platform, you want to reach out as far as you possibly can. While there are certainly many vintage clothes enthusiasts out there, as the sisters already knew, they needed to think about what other areas of expertise they might have that they weren't focusing on. So, I asked them "What do you know?" It turns out that running a vintage clothing store requires quite a bit more than a knowledge of secondhand clothes. Here's a list of items that came to mind when I thought of the sisters. I thought about what kinds of skills were used in running the shop, topics and trends in the news that pertained to their skills, as well as any areas that were unique to their own personalities.

- small businesses
- business savvy
- women in business
- fashion
- *Project Runway* fans
- designer labels

- people skills
- Brooklyn
- Miami
- style
- style on a budget
- accessories
- women expressing themselves through their personal style

Identify Your Pockets of Focus

As you may be able to see from the list, a few very distinctive patterns emerged. I felt that their areas of expertise could be grouped into a few "pockets of focus." While it is crucial to reach beyond your most obvious area of expertise, you don't want to be spreading yourself too thin, nor do you want to be grasping at straws. These pockets of focus are going to take you to places where you are going to search for your audience, so you want to make sure you're going places that make sense—places where you feel comfortable. You also want to make sure these pockets are concrete enough. While it's always okay to toss anything that comes to mind on a list while brainstorming, something that's too vague just isn't going to work for a platform. For instance, "people skills" was just too vague. Yes, these sisters have them, and it's an essential quality for platform building, but I couldn't think of a way to translate this skill into an actual audience, so it didn't make the cut. Ultimately, Melissa and Alison's list looked like this:

- small business (including women in business)
- designer clothes (they deal with high-end stuff too, so the upper echelon of fashion should be part of their market)
- style on a budget (what better way to save money than by buying vintage?)
- travel, Miami, Brooklyn, New York City

Who Do I Know?

While you do know more people than you realize, I'm asking you "who you know" in a more figurative way. While friends and family are an essential resource when it comes to building a platform, right now we're going to talk about all of the wonderful people out there who are just dying to buy your book. Who are these people? Where do you find them? They are all out there—attached to one of those elements you came up with when you developed your pockets of focus. I realize this can be a little overwhelming at first, but most writers find this process very energizing. It can be exciting to see the edges of that platform taking shape! Here are a few pointers to get you started and to make the process a little less daunting:

- Go ahead and start by looking at your actual personal contact list. Who do you know that might be able to help? Make organized lists of who can help and how.
- Think outside the address book. Do you recall a conversation with an aunt or neighbor who knew someone who knew someone? It might be worth asking to see if a connection can be made.
- Break down each pocket of focus into actionable steps. What organizations exist that you can contact? Do you know anyone in that organization? Do they publish a newsletter? If so, get it! Do they have a website? Do they hold fundraisers, cocktail parties? Do they need speakers?
- Seek connecters. As you're searching for venues, are there any names that come up as to people you should meet? If so, be sure to meet them!
- Are there conferences aimed toward people who are interested in your topic? Can you attend? Can you speak at the conference? If not, do they have a blog or website that will enable you to connect with attendees?

> **QUICK TIP:** *Label people! Yes, I know. We're not supposed to use labels. But this is only temporary and it's just to keep you organized I promise! For instance, if you are writing a memoir about baking cakes in France, go through your contact list and make a mark for people who like cake (I know, this includes everyone right?), people who love memoirs in general, and lastly, one for Francophiles. It can help you target e-mails, marketing materials, newsletters, invitations, or anything else you might send out related to your book.*

Again, to use Alison and Melissa as an example, they could have targeted the large fashion magazines, both high-end and funky fashion blogs, any publications or organizations for small businesses, as well as any organizations that exist pertaining to particular events that might be going on in Miami and Brooklyn. There are so many opportunities here—countless people to meet, an endless list of blogs to target, lots of events to attend, etc. It's exciting to see that there are so many possibilities. But how do you effectively use these places to help build your platform? How do you make an impact?

What Can I Do?

You know with certainty what you're good at, and you have a solid list of people who can be helpful, as well as a growing file of organizations, publications, blogs, websites, and so on that pertain to the platform you want to build. So, where do you begin? By cloning yourself so you can get it all done somehow? I know it seems overwhelming and you're praying that a staff of twelve will magically show up on your doorstep baring skinny lattes and cell phones to take care of everything, but I assure you that with a plan, this is totally doable. Broken down into manageable sections and fit into a schedule that works for you, you'll soon see that by spending a small amount of time working on your platform each day can yield big results. The key is planning, consistency, and patience.

The Three Point Plan

Like any big project, it helps to have a plan in place. I always find it immensely helpfully when launching a big project if there are a few things on a massive to-do list that I can do immediately without much effort. Yes, it's possible that one of the items on that list might be "meet best friend for coffee and support," but that's okay. I've managed to cross off one item. Breaking your plan down as follows can help you feel energized about your platform, help you to see the end goal (Selling books! Impressing agents and publishers!), and of course, keep you organized and on track:

THREE POINT PLAN	WRITING AND SELLING YOUR MEMOIR
Things I can do now.	Start a blog, new Twitter account, meet people on blogosphere, start commenting on blogs. Blog 2x per week, research writers conferences.
Things I can do later.	Blog at least 3x per week after finish manuscript, teach class?, start seminars?, enter writing contests. Facebook page, Squidoo page. Host an event. Network with booksellers. Guest post on blogs.
Future goals and maintenance.	Become go-to person on memoir writing and regular speaker at conferences. Speak at mom conferences about memoir writing. Increase blog traffic. Get 1,000+ Twitter followers. Become a columnist.

My chart is of course a general overview of my plans—a way to make sense of the pile of information on my desk (and in my

lling your memoir

head). You may very well want to make more detailed notes, but my point here is that you think about what you can do now, what tasks might require more time to develop, and equally important, now that you've found that audience, how are you going to keep them?

RECOMMENDED READING

BOOKS TO HELP DEVELOP A PLATFORM

Get Known Before the Book Deal: Use Your Personal Strengths to Grow an Author Platform by Christina Katz

How to Become a Famous Writer Before You're Dead by Ariel Gore

CHAPTER TWELVE:

Social Media: The Best Thing to Come Along for Writers Since Coffee

U ntil fairly recently, I thought Facebook was only good for connecting with long lost friends from high school and posting pictures of my kid looking especially adorable in her Halloween costume. I had absolutely no interest in Twitter. Why would anyone care when and where I'm drinking my coffee? Does anyone really want an "update" on what I'm feeling on an hour-by-hour or minute-by-minute basis? And blogs? Who has time to read the random rants of disgruntled twenty-somethings? I assumed Facebook was for communicating with distant cousins, Twitter was for kids, and blogs were for people with too much time on their hands. I know now that I was very, very wrong. If used properly, social media can be incredibly helpful for writers. It's a terrific way to connect with potential readers, network with other writers, stay in the know, and yes, help develop and expand that ever important platform. Not to mention, there's some great material to read out there. And best of all? The social media that you choose to use is all completely under *your* control, and totally free. With social media, there's no waiting for an editor's approval on a story you've pitched, waiting to hear back from a producer on a TV show about a segment, or waiting to see if you'll be invited to speak at a conference. The results you get out of social media are a direct result of the efforts you put in. So where do you begin?

THE WILD WORLD OF BLOGGING

The best thing about blogging? Anyone can do it! The worst thing about blogging? *Anyone* can do it. This means that while starting a blog is a relatively easy and painless experience, there are so many blogs out there today that you can't make a splash with a blog without some serious thought and effort. However, you don't actually have to be a blogger to enjoy the many benefits of the blogosphere. And while I think there are quite a few advantages to starting one, keep in mind that knowing how to navigate the blogosphere and actually blogging are two different things. What exactly does that mean for you? It means that if you plan to use the blogosphere as part of your platform-launching initiatives, you need to make a decision about which approach you want to take.

Do You Want to Be a Blogger?

Blogging can be a wonderful tool, and it's especially conducive to memoir writers who are already accustomed to writing about personal issues and aren't afraid to put themselves out there. But know that to be a successful blogger is to be an informed blogger. With countless blogs floating around on the internet already, what can you do to draw new readers? It is essential, just as it is with planning your memoir, that you stop and think about what's missing. What's already out there? What can you add to the mix? Blogs also require a constant production of content, which means lots of work—make sure these efforts are worth your time and that you're contributing something that is fresh and new. That being said, the pressure to produce content on a regular basis can be a fantastic exercise for a writer. Publicly putting your work up for an audience on a regular basis means that you're honing your skills, getting feedback, and most importantly, you're writing! Following are a few tips on creating a successful blog:

Elements of a Successful Blog

- **FREQUENT POSTS.** You won't attract a following if you randomly post a few times per month. Post frequently and regularly so that your readers know what to expect.

- **QUALITY CONTENT.** Think about the quality of the posts you're putting up, as they reflect on you. Will this information be of interest to your audience? Do you have something to offer that other bloggers just aren't covering? Ask yourself before posting. Will this piece get readers coming back to my blog?

- **DESIGN.** You by no means need to be a graphic designer or even have special computer programs to add personality to your blog. Free sites, like wordpress.com, offer countless templates that you can customize with images and fonts that represent your own sense of style.

- **NICHE.** Is there a particular area of your memoir that lends itself to a blog? Conjure up your inner Julie Powell. Imagine if she had done a blog on "bored secretaries who are dissatisfied with their jobs and lives so they cook a lot" rather than focused her blog specifically on her project, which was working her way through *Mastering the Art of French Cooking*. If the topic of your memoir is bigger than the topic of your blog, that's fine, but don't be too broad with your blog topic. Think niche.

- **COMMUNITY.** What do you have to offer? Being a blogger means being part of the blogosphere. If you want traffic, you need to get out there and get it. Post comments on other sites, participate in conversations. Attend a blogging conference and meet some like-minded bloggers. Offer to write a guest post on a blog that you like that has a similar sensibility. The blogosphere is about generosity. Spread it!

> **QUICK TIP:** *If you're interesting in blogging, but are intimidated by the idea of producing content on a daily or almost daily basis, consider starting a blog with a couple of like-minded writers. As a new mom, I knew I couldn't handle the pressure of daily posts but was really attracted to the idea of blogging. Luckily, I knew two other moms who were in the exact same boat as I was. That's how ad hoc MOM was born. If Carrie, Tonya, and I didn't work together, the content just wouldn't be there. We are also able to share marketing efforts and can adjust the editorial schedule to fit everyone's needs. It works!*

Navigating the Blogosphere as a Non-Blogger

Blogging just isn't for everyone. Undeniably it takes a lot of time, and blogging is best entered into with a proper plan once you're prepared to start updating your blog on a regular basis. But the blogosphere still has much to offer even if you aren't a blogger. There are blogs written on every topic under the sun, and I guarantee that unless your memoir is about your trip to outer space, there will be many good blogs on a topic similar to the one you're writing about. You can spend some time getting to know the various blogs with similar topics and decide which ones might be helpful to you. How do you know? Here are a few things to keep in mind:

- The content of the blog speaks to you and is a natural complement to your memoir.
- The writer updates their content frequently.
- The blogger appears to be part of an active community.
- The blog seems to have a steady following of readers.

Check, check, and check! What next? Become a faithful reader. Leave comments. Pay attention to who else leaves comments. Is there someone leaving comments who has an interesting voice? Do you want to check out their blog? Most bloggers tend to truly value their faithful readers. If you read the blog every day and leave a thoughtful comment, you'll essentially be developing a relationship with that entire community. Once you've done that, you'll be able to simply introduce yourself—many bloggers have their e-mail addresses listed—and tell them about your upcoming book. You'll be surprised by how far this relationship can reach. That being said, don't think you can get to know someone via blog for two weeks and then just throw out the "hey, promote my book" line. The blogosphere is about spreading generosity all around. It's about getting to know people and helping each other, not just using people for the convenience of promoting *your* book.

> **QUICK TIP:** *The blogosphere can be an overwhelming place. When I started searching for blogs that interested me, I stumbled upon countless blogs that I liked. Initially, I was trying to comment daily on twenty-five blogs. I just couldn't do it! Start by choosing three to five blogs that you truly love. Develop those relationships first and then branch out.*

TWITTER: NOT JUST FOR TELLING PEOPLE ABOUT THE WONDERFUL CABERNET YOU'RE DRINKING

I attended a conference of bloggers not too long ago where I swear I was the only one out of about 2,500 women who was *not* on Twitter. I found this shocking. Until that moment, I had assumed that Twitter was for college kids. That "tweets" consisted of announcements, such as "I'm having an awesome night" or for thirteen year olds who have to frequently proclaim their love for Justin Bieber electronically. But this conference was full of professional women.

Writers, marketers, advertisers—every one of whom had a Twitter account. How did I not know this? And what exactly were they tweeting about and how did they use Twitter to their advantage? After a crash course in Twitter, I immediately saw how this application could be a huge asset to writers, for platform-building purposes, networking, and of course book selling.

If you're writing a memoir about wine, then by all means tweet about wine. I just wanted to point out that it's a common misconception that Twitter is just a vehicle for sharing the totally mundane details of everyone's lives. Do some people insist on sharing the fact that they're "kicking back with a beer" or "eating a cookie?" Well, yes. That might be interesting to people if you're Madonna, but not so if you're, well, you or me. Twitter is about providing readers with interesting, relevant, and timely information to your core group of followers. Think about the topic of your memoir. Think about your hook. Who is going to be interested? What kinds of information are people seeking? It's about identifying those people and providing the information they're looking for. How do you do this?

By now, everyone knows about the wild success story of *Sh*t My Dad Says* by Justin Halpern. A #1 *New York Times* best-selling memoir, a CBS TV show starring William Shatner, all born from a Twitter account. And while I think it's unlikely that Twitter accounts will be launching many book deals, I bring this up to show you that, used creatively, Twitter does have the power to reach an incredibly large number of people.

If You Don't Tweet About Wine, What Do You Tweet About?

If you're writing a memoir about wine, then by all means tweet about wine. I just wanted to point out that it's a common misconception that Twitter is just a vehicle for sharing the totally mundane details of everyone's lives. Do some people insist on sharing the fact that they're "kicking back with a beer" or "eating a cookie?" Well, yes. That might be interesting to people if you're Madonna, but not so if you're, well, you or me. Twitter is about providing readers with interesting, relevant, and timely information to your core group of followers. Think about the topic of your memoir. Think about your hook. Who is going to be interested? What kinds of information are people seeking? It's about identifying those people and providing the information they're looking for. How do you do this?

Twitter: The Step-by-Step Guide

1) **SIGN UP FOR AN TWITTER.COM ACCOUNT** and select a Twitter name. Keep the name interesting, but short. Why? Your tweets are limited to 140 characters, but I suggest you only use 120 of them (more on that soon), so don't waste them on your name.

2) **WRITE YOUR BIO.** This is overlooked and important. If you want followers, they need to know what it is you're interested in. Flowers? Chocolate? Do you tweet about politics? Parenting? If you have a blog or website, be sure to include this information.

3) **A PHOTO OR PICTURE IS KEY!** The pictures that Twitter automatically provides send a message that you're a newbie, or just not that interested. Upload a picture or an image to create a unique feel for your page and to start creating a brand for yourself.

4) **START SEARCHING FOR PEOPLE TO FOLLOW.** Who tweets on a similar subject matter? How frequently do they tweet? Are their tweets good quality? Are they providing good information or announcing what they had for lunch? Are they including links to relevant articles? How often are they tweeting?

5) **SEND YOUR FIRST TWEET!** Your first one might be an introduction. Then start to send relevant information. Articles, links, whatever would be interesting to the people who follow you or who you would like to have follow you.

> **QUICK TIP:** *When searching for people to follow on Twitter, look at their timeline of tweets. Hint: You might want to think twice about someone who is tweeting all day long. It can be annoying to see the same person popping into your Twitter account over and over. Anyone who is Tweeting more than once an hour or more than five times a day might be overdoing it.*

How Does Twitter Ultimately Help?

What exactly is the meaning of all this? What is the point of taking the time to find, and tweet out relevant information to people you don't actually know? Should you care about creating a group of "followers?" I mean, you stopped caring about being popular back in high school right? I hear what you're saying and know it all sounds strange. Think of it this way: Twitter is not so much a popularity contest as it is a means of branding yourself. Twitter provides an easy and, remember, free way to show the world (or a pretty large portion of it) how much you know about your area of expertise. Twitter provides a perfect opportunity to use your voice, albeit in just a few characters, to send out exciting, unusual, creative, and imaginative bits of information that no one else is sending out on your topic. By becoming an expert in your area, you'll be increasing your reach, gaining more followers, and ultimately, helping develop your platform. This is an incredibly helpful tool that will help support any of your endeavors. You can tweet about events you want to promote or articles you're writing; you can look for sources, throw out ideas, and yes, eventually someday, tweet about your book. Twitter is changing every day, and it's always wise with anything that's done online to keep yourself up-to-date by investigating the latest trends—online. What better way to stay in the know? However, as of now, there are some cardinal no-break rules and a few other helpful hints you should know to get you started. Learning to use Twitter is like learning another language. It takes a little floundering before you become fluent. You just have to jump in and know you'll get used to it before long.

> **QUICK TIP:** *If you want your tweet to receive the coveted "retweet" by another follower, never use your full 140 characters. Use just 120. I'm much more apt to retweet something when I don't have to spend a lot of time fiddling with the text of a tweet. This makes it more challenging to write a tweet, but trust me, it's worth it to get the extra attention you get from a retweet.*

The Cardinal Rules of Twitter

- Tweet three to five times a day. That's enough; be exclusive!
- Never tweet more than once per hour. Seriously, don't be a pesty Twitterer!
- Ask yourself (I'm begging you here), does this fall into the category of TMI (too much information)? If there is even the slightest question that it does, *don't* tweet it.
- Make sure your information is interesting, relevant, and timely. Do your readers want to know about whatever it is you are sending?
- Don't send superfluous tweets, such as the "good morning Twitter" or "Good night Twitterverse" tweet. Annoying and so unnecessary.

- Double check before you direct message someone that you aren't in fact "tweeting at them." Is the "d" before their name? Make sure!

Twitter Mysteries Solved

Retweeting, tweeting "at someone," direct messages, Hootsuite, Tweetdeck, etc. There are loads of helpful tools and resources to make tweeting easier and to keep your tweets organized. You can even set up your tweets in advance! I happen to find this trick especially helpful and was greatly relieved to discover I wouldn't have to spend the majority of my time sitting in front of the computer. I've listed some resources at the end of this chapter that can help sort out some of the confusion around various applications, Twitter etiquette, and just generally help you get started. Have fun and enjoy.

FACEBOOK: NOT JUST FOR LONG LOST HIGH SCHOOL SWEETHEARTS

The bottom line is that different people are more comfortable looking at different applications online. It's been my experience that some people will look at a blog faithfully every day, while others aren't big blog readers, but they will read material you put up on your Facebook page. While it may seem like a complicated extra step to take every day, it is worth your time to make a Facebook page that complements the platform you are creating. Think of it as insurance for your platform—it's just another way of making sure you're using every possible means to reach your core audience. Facebook, just like Twitter, makes it easy for you to upload images or photos so that you can personalize your page in order to carry across the look you've chosen to represent your platform. Keep in mind that being consistent with your look is important. You want your readers to be able to recognize you wherever they happen to stumble upon you on the internet.

AND WHATEVER ELSE WILL BE INVENTED: A FEW WORDS ABOUT STAYING CURRENT

Technology changes fast and frequently. And while it appears that Facebook and Twitter are here to stay, there's bound to be something new and exciting popping up on the scene anytime now. My advice to you is USE IT! Learn from your kids or your neighbor's kids. If you don't know any kids, borrow one. Technology is so helpful—it's accessible to everyone, and again, it's free. When something is free that means there's room for experimentation. How often do we get to do that? You've worked hard and you owe it to yourself to draw attention to your work. So why not take advantage of these wonderful tools that are out there for the taking?

RECOMMENDED READING

SOCIAL MEDIA RESOURCES TO GET YOU STARTED
www.sreetips.com
www.getinthehotspot.com/
http://blog.penelopetrunk.com/penelopes-guide-to-blogging

CHAPTER THIRTEEN:

Everything You Always Wanted to Know About Literary Agents and How to Get One

T his is the big question writers always wants to know the answer to. How do you get an agent? Do you have to be related to one? Sell your soul? Do you have to get them on the phone and just *convince them* to read your work? If they could hear your passion coming through the line, they would certainly be able to tell how great of a writer you are, right? Or should you show up at their office with your manuscript and a big smile? Or wait! Send a gift? Call repeatedly about two weeks after you stuck your query in the mail (so they know you're serious)? Well, I'm going to tell you something. There *is* a secret to getting a literary agent. Are you ready? Get out a highlighter, because I'm about to tell you what it is. Here it goes:

THE SECRET TO LANDING A LITERARY AGENT

1. Submit a well-written letter and quality pages.
2. Do your research.
3. Behave like someone who is about to enter into a business relationship.

Sounds simple, right? In fact, you are probably disappointed—as if I don't have any actual wisdom to impart. But if you listen carefully to what I'm about to tell you, and actually follow it, you will be in an excellent position to get a literary agent. *I swear.* While what I've outlined sounds simple, any agent will tell you that it is incredibly rare that someone actually follows this formula. The majority of the packages or letters that agents receive are poorly written, the pages are not ready to be seen by anyone other than the writer's best friend or immediate family, the writer is not be-having like someone we would want to do business with, and more often than not, the project in question is not even a good match for us. It's up to you. It is completely in your power to cre-ate a good submission package. And I guarantee you that when agents get a good one, it's not unusual for us to actually stop what we're doing to read. I get hundreds of submissions every month, and months go by without my requesting additional pages from an author. So trust me, I'm positively delighted to get something that's well presented and piques my interest. So how do you go about doing that?

Quality Pages: Are You Truly Ready for This? Seriously, Are You?

We talked about being "an almost" in chapter ten, but it's worth going over again. Remember, while an agent will certainly add his two cents to a manuscript or proposal, he is not going to take the scraps of your memoir and help you construct something from nothing. Your pages need to be the best they can possibly be before you should even think of sending them out. If you can identify with any of the following statements, DO NOT SEND YOUR PAGES OUT TO AN AGENT.

1. I could probably do one more round of revisions, but I just want an agent's opinion before I do any more work.
2. My mom thinks it's pretty good, so I'm going to send it out, even though everyone in my writers' group thought I should wait.

3. It's a really great idea, but I don't think it's worth it to me to take the time to write more unless an agent thinks they can sell it.

4. I'll have some pages ready in about six months, but it's hard to get an agent, so I'm going to start querying now.

5. I think my pages are really good, but I'm a terrible copyeditor, so I guess I'll just do my best and hope I catch my mistakes.

Again, if you feel like any one of those statements describes you, then STOP. Do not send out your pages. A simple polish can make all the difference so ask a friend with a sharp eye to look for typos. I know writing can be an exhausting process, and you're anxious for a professional opinion, but if you want a professional opinion on pages that aren't ready, I guarantee you that the opinion you're seeking is going to come via a form rejection letter that says "no thanks." Is that the kind of opinion you really want? Take pride in your work. When you think it's there, put it away for a day or two, look again, and be doubly sure. If this is your first foray into the world of literary agents, why not make it a successful experience rather than one marred by rejection slips and regrets about how you should have revised a little bit more?

WELL-WRITTEN QUERY LETTERS: MISSPELLED NAMES AND THE MYTH OF THE WORD COUNT

There are two easily avoided things that will label you a newbie as soon as an agent gets your query letter. The first is to whom you address the letter. Seriously, it's not that hard to spell my name right—or to use the right one. There is another literary agent out there whose last name also begins with the letter "B." I get at least two queries addressed to her at my agency every month. Those queries go right in the trash. I'm also frequently addressed as "Paula Blazer," "Paula Belzer," and my favorite "Mr. Paul Balzer." I realize that absolutely everyone makes mistakes. And here's a confession: I myself am a terrible copyeditor. But I know this! I have to ask someone I trust to review my work carefully before I send it out. There's no shame in not having a keen eye for typos, but that means you have to take extra steps to ensure you're not sending your pages out the door with embarrassing mistakes that are going to land your query letter right in the trash.

The second way to give away your novice status is in the myth of the word count. I'd say about 90 percent of the queries I receive start with a precise word count of the manuscript. Within the first few sentences, the author feels a need to point out that she's "written a memoir of 82,403 words that details her experiences living in a tree house." I've asked around, and we agents are baffled by this. Who decided that writers need to tell us how many words their manuscript is? And right up top in those precious first few sentences where they should be wowing us with their prose, platform, and amazing book idea? My eyes positively glaze over whenever I see that word count lying there, taking up perfectly good space on top of a query letter. It's just not necessary. That being said, what you do need to know is this: An important part of being ready to submit your work means having a "book-length work" that is ready to go. A book-length work varies, but is generally 70,000 to 90,000 words. Of course, some books are slightly shorter, and they can be much longer—and this is probably where this mentioning of the word count originally stemmed from. But since you are a savvy, in-the-know kind of person, your manuscript will be well within that range and there will be no need to include a word count in your query. There is much better use of that precious space!

The Anatomy of a Good Query Letter

So how do you write a query letter that catches an agent's attention? The key here is to write a letter that captures the tone of your work, highlights your voice, and also manages to give the agent a sense of what your platform is. You want to share your idea, show off your style, and also point out that there is a reason as to why you are the perfect person to write this particular book. It sounds daunting to be sure, but many writers find that they know their material so well that writing the query letter isn't all that hard with the right guidance. It's just a matter of knowing how to funnel the right information onto the page. Here are some general guidelines to familiarize yourself with before we get into the specifics:

- Query letters should be one page long.
- Don't make me guess what it is you're writing. It should quickly become clear whether it's a memoir, novel, work of nonfiction, etc.
- Always include a self-addressed, stamped return envelope.
- Include your contact information. This sounds obvious, but you'd be surprised what people forget to do.
- Double-space your sample chapters if you are permitted to include them and use a 12 point font. If an agent doesn't specify what "sample chapters" constitutes, approximately fifty pages is a good rule of thumb.

QUICK TIP: *It's often difficult to figure out how many query letters to send out at once. I would recommend starting with approximately six or so. You want to test the waters—see how your work is received. That being said, as you're researching potential agents, feel free to create an "A-list" and a "B-list." Start querying your A-list agents and work your way down. It's not wise to submit to every agent on your list, only to find that your query isn't yielding the results you want and you need to change it.*

The Opener: Who Are You? Do I Know You? Why Should I Spend Five Minutes Reading Your Letter?

Your opener is your opportunity to use any connections you may have to the agent you are querying. Did you meet him or her at a conference? Were you referred by someone? Who? Did the agent meet you at the playground? If you have a personal connection to the agent, while you shouldn't be afraid to use it, please keep in mind that it doesn't mean you should call them on the phone or invite them to your house for dinner. I'm simply saying that if you've met an agent or they should be expecting your work, they may need a reminder to help make the connection. "Right! I remember that my Aunt Janice said that her neighbor's daughter-in-law was going to send along her chapters." We all have relatives that we don't want to anger.

What If I Just Don't Know "Anybody?"

Fear not! I know the feeling. I didn't know a soul when I moved here from the Midwest, and it was incredibly intimidating applying for jobs in book publishing without any connections. In fact, I wouldn't have gotten my first job at a literary agency had a friend of mine not gotten into a car accident with an editor at a major publishing house. How crazy is that? She was uninjured in the accident in case you were tossing this book aside in disgust and cursing me for being an opportunist. But please know that there are countless authors who make their way in the world of publishing without any connections or experience with writing. While I have already urged you to work on your platform before sending out queries, and I'm sure you've begun to make great strides in that department, don't feel defeated if your list of contacts doesn't include a long list of New York City editors and agents. With tenacity and hard work, you'll get there. But what do you say in the opening paragraph of your letter if you haven't met the agent you're querying or you don't have a personal connection?

Tactic #1: Make a Connection

It isn't crucial to have met the agent you want to submit your work to. If fact, if I think back on my client list, there are very few clients I have actually met prior to representing them. So how did the connection happen? They made it happen by referencing a previous book of mine that was either similar in tone to their work, or which they liked. Please don't think that means that every single agent (myself included) needs to have their butt kissed in order to look at your query. I'm simply saying that if someone has a genuine interest in a book of mine, and they can sincerely convey that in a letter, it shows that the author took the time to research what I do and what my tastes are. That being said, this tactic obviously doesn't work if the writer is trying to force a connection that just isn't there. If you're approaching an agent who has a great track record of selling spiritual memoirs with your memoir about the year you spent selling drugs on your college campus, you can flatter them as much as you like—your memoir just isn't likely to fall into the type of book they know how to sell. It's nothing personal.

Tactic #2: Be Seductive

Sometimes it's best to just use your wiles and seduce the agent with a sentence or two about your project. What makes your project so irresistible? Why should it be published? Why is it better than anything else that's out there right now? Why are you the person to write it? You may want to borrow a sentence or two from your actual book to use for this section, but be sure to limit yourself. You want to be able to explain quickly that you're writing a memoir. You don't want the agent wondering if you're writing a memoir, novel, or short story collection.

The Body of the Letter:
Lean on Your Hook to Tell Your Story

The body of your letter should continue telling your story, but briefly, succinctly, and in the same tone your memoir is written in. This is key. I can't tell you how many letters I get that are written in a very businesslike fashion, yet the story they are proposing sounds like fun, and I can't possibly begin to imagine how these two styles would possibly go together. Be sure to mirror the tone you use in your memoir in your letter—and lean on your hook to draw the agent in. What is the hook of your book? Remember how your hook was that something special that made your story stand out from all of the other ones on the shelf? This is the perfect time to explain how your story is unique. Keep this section compelling—yet short and simple.

The Closer: Make Me Want to Call You

My eyes often drift down to the ending of a letter once I sense that it's going to be a good one. That's because I know that the bottom of the letter is where I'm going to find any information about writing credits, professional affiliations, prior books that have been written, TV experience, or anything especially interesting about you. Be sure to clearly state and include everything related to your platform and any relevant experience that ties into the writing of this book. Agents need help promoting you to a publisher, so be sure to do your job and make sure that you have lots of helpful items to fill this paragraph up with!

THE MAJOR MISMATCH: A LITTLE RESEARCH GOES A LONG WAY

A huge percentage of the submissions in my slush pile are immediately dismissed because the books that writers are pitching me are completely wrong for my list. This isn't entirely the author's fault, as there are many websites and guidebooks that just aren't 100 per-cent accurate (whoever said I do historical fiction, you are totally wrong!), however, a little additional research would have helped these authors create a much more appropriate list of agents to query. My list focuses on fiction (but not sci-fi, YA, historical, romance, or fantasy), popular culture, memoir, and journalism. So imagine my surprise every single week as I receive a mailbox full of queries for illustrated books, children's books, cartoons, screenplays, plays, YA novels, historical fiction, sci-fi, fantasy, horror, and graphic novels. Had these authors done just a bit more research, they would have saved quite a bit of money on photocopies and stamps. However, my all-time favorite group of submissions comes from fans of E. Lynn Harris. I don't represent E. Lynn Harris, however I've had the pleasure of working with a wonderful writer named Lynn Harris, *no* "E." It took me about two minutes to confirm who actually rep-resents the late Mr. E. Lynn Harris. So why do so many writers out there who put together submission packages and query letters fail to take the extra time to confirm they are sending their work to the right person? Because it is easy to forget that the submission process, the publishing process, and every part of your career that *relates to writing* is as equally important as the writing itself. Just remember, writing is a job, and it's crucial that you do all of it well.

Research Backwards

The mistake many writers make is that they research agents. They start looking up names of agents and agencies, looking at what they do, getting their addresses, and sending off their materials. I know that, on the surface, this makes sense. Agents perform the services you seek. However, getting an agent isn't quite like hiring a plumber. You wake up with a flooded basement and basically you need some-one who is reliable, available, and well, a plumber. Agenting doesn't work that way. It's about making a proper match. It's crucial that you find one that you click with. You need to have similar tastes, you need to communicate well, work well together, the agents needs to be ready and willing to take on your project, and you have to *like each other.* You don't have to like your plumber that much (although I imagine it's a plus if you do). It isn't essential to the fixing of your pipes that you and your plumber have the same tastes in anything at all. So how do you go about finding this person? How are you possibly going to tell whether or not you're going to "click" with an agent from a guidebook? Well, you're not. That's why you need to "research backwards." It's a simple and positively old-fashioned method of finding an agent and despite all of the developments in technology and social media, researching backwards remains the best way to find an agent who is likely to connect with your work. I'm going to outline the general process for you:

STEP #1:
What Books Have the Same Essence as Yours?

Think of a few books that have a similar essence to your book. For instance, if you've written a quirky memoir that is very funny, you might write down the following titles. I'm going to use three for this exercise, but I'd suggest doing more for your agent search. Don't limit yourself to huge bestsellers for examples either. Use a mixture of big books and those that you love that aren't hugely successful.

- *Mennonite in a Little Black Dress* by Rhoda Janzen
- *A Girl Named Zippy* by Haven Kimmel
- *Slackjaw* by Jim Knipfel

STEP #2:
Visit the Local Bookstore

Is there anything new on the shelf that also inspires you and that you feel is similar in essence to your memoir? Is there anything on the recommended reading shelf that appeals to you? It may also be a good idea to look for books that are turned out on the bookshelves. I also love to check out the "staff picks" section to see if there is anything inspiring that I'm not familiar with. Add any titles that appeal to you to your list.

> **QUICK TIP:** *Making friends with a local bookseller is a great way to get book recommendations. I knew a bookseller at an independent store who never failed to find the perfect book for my moods. I could tell her I wanted something light, silly, girly, and urban—she'd find the right book. I could go back the next week for something mysterious and dramatic, and she'd know exactly what to give me. As a result, I spent quite a lot of money at her store, but it was well worth it!*

STEP #3:
Read the Acknowledgments

More often than not, authors will thank their agents in the acknowledgments section of their memoir, which may be listed in the front or the back of the book. Do some authors totally skip acknowledgments sections all together? Yes—but usually they don't. Once you see the agents listed in the acknowledgments of the books you've selected, you can research those agents as well. A quick Internet search will give you information about where they work, what other kinds of books they represent, and often, you'll find information about their submission requirements. If the author has not included an acknowledgments page, an Internet search will often tell you who the agent is. This truly is the best way to find appropriate agents to query. Sending out query letters is hard work, so you want to make sure your efforts are well thought through. Agents appreciate it, too. We much prefer to get queries about topics that interest us than letters about genres of books we've simply never represented. It's also nice to open a letter to

read, "I'm querying you because I so loved your book *Candy Girl*"—
we just never get tired of hearing our work complimented.

ACT LIKE SOMEONE YOU'D WANT TO DO BUSINESS WITH

Why You Should Never Call an Agent. EVER.

If you are trying to get an agent, do NOT call them on the phone.
I repeat, the *worst* thing you can do during this process is call an
agent on the phone. I'm sure you're perfectly lovely, but I promise
that whoever told you that if you "just get them on the phone, you'll
be able to convince them that you're book will be huge" was doing
you a massive disservice. We really don't want to spend our time
answering questions about your submission. If you do have a question about the submission process that you can't find the answer
to online, DO YOUR BEST TO FIGURE IT OUT. The thing is, a
submission to an agent is kind of like a quiz. If you do a reasonably
good job of it, it's only going to help your overall grade. While yes,
agents have preferred ways of receiving things, I don't happen to
know anyone who is so particular about it that they're going to toss
out a submission they're interested in, just because it's in Helvetica
font and not Times New Roman. No agent in their right mind is going to say, "Wow, this manuscript is the best memoir I've read since
The Glass Castle! In fact, I think it's even better! Too bad she sent
four sample chapters instead of three. That just isn't following my
policy. I know I could sell this for six-figures, but because she didn't
follow my personal eccentric rules regarding submissions, I'm going
to forfeit any potential riches for myself and throw this in the trash
and send her a form rejection letter instead." Trust me. This just isn't
going to happen. If there was an agent who behaved in such a way,
I dare say you wouldn't want them representing you.

Please keep all of this in mind before you pick up the phone to ask any of the following questions:

- "Are you accepting query letters?"
- "Do you want sample chapters?"
- *The Literary Marketplace* says you accept sample chapters. How many pages is that?"
- "How long will it take for you to get back to me?"
- "I've written a book do you want to see it?"

Even if you're debating sample chapters versus no sample chapters, just take a guess—BUT DON'T CALL. Getting more sample chapters than we'd like is a million times less annoying than getting the call asking if we want them. Trust me on this one. And more importantly, trust yourself! If you've figured out how to write an entire book proposal or manuscript, chances are you're a pretty smart cookie and you can navigate this part of the game just fine. Remember the magical recipe for getting an agent? If you've followed item #1 (submit a well-written query and quality pages) and item #2 (you did your research), it's time to remember item #3 and act like a person who is about to enter into a business relationship. That means not being pesky and being respectful of someone else's time. What I'm telling you is that there is a code of behavior here, and I'm urging you to follow it by sitting back, working on your writing, and having faith that if an agent wants to represent you, they will get in touch with you. It takes patience, my friend. Stick those pages in the mail, sit back, read a book, or start thinking long and hard about what you're going to write next.

The More Basic Your Package the Better

We don't want anything fancy at all—seriously, we don't. That means we don't want chocolate, candy, or flowers. As much as I love a good chocolate fix come 4 P.M., getting a present from a complete stranger who wants to secure your services just comes off as weird. Don't do it. Please stick to the following guidelines when preparing your submission packages. Trust me, keeping things simple makes your package stand out *in a good way.*

- Don't use so much tape and packing material (really, are packing peanuts necessary?) that I can't open your manuscript. You would be surprised how many people do this. Seriously people! It's paper!
- Don't send flowers or some such other gift. It's totally creepy.
- Don't use a freakishly small font (we're all half blind).
- Don't single-space your manuscript (see previous comment regarding eyesight).
- Don't punch holes in your pages and stick them in a giant binder. Unwieldy!
- Don't print on both sides of the paper.
- Don't handwrite your letter or submission, unless you are writing from prison. (By the way, I'm totally serious here.)
- Don't include your word count.
- Don't use colored paper or colored ink.
- Don't include pictures, a mock-up of a cover, a CD, or a DVD.
- Avoid cheesy letterhead featuring quills, typewriters, and pens.

When Your Query Isn't Getting Results

If you're doing your job right, I would say one out of every three agents you query should ask to see your work. But what if you're only getting back form rejection letters? Then it's time to revisit your query letter. What isn't working? Start by double-checking the basics. Are the names spelled correctly? Is your query well copy-edited? If you're sending out a clean letter, then it's time to focus on content. What about your letter isn't grabbing people? Is it too wordy? Is it too difficult to tell what your story is about? Is your hook buried too far into the letter? What about your platform? How solid does it sound? Are you able to list a few items or just one? Does it come off as solid or weak? Spend a day or two analyzing your letter and how both you and your project look on paper. Think about what you can do to improve the situation and move onto the next names on your list.

> **QUICK TIP:** *Avoid Desperate Writer Syndrome! It is a major turnoff when a writer starts off a letter with the "I have five books to show you" line. How does an agent interpret this? That you have a drawer full of unpublishable work, and you want us to do something with it. No thanks! We're also nervous when a letter starts off with a list of agents who have previously represented you (read, you're difficult), or you've submitted your book to every major publisher (what's left for us to do with it?). Think long and hard about the impression you're making when you talk about your previous experiences with agents, publishers, and unpublished works. Is this the best way to start off a new relationship?*

WHEN AN AGENT CALLS

An agent has called me and offered me representation! I have to just say yes, right? I mean, who am I to ask them anything? I should just ignore everyone else I approached and go with them? This is what I've been waiting for, isn't it? I did actually really want to sign with Agent X the most, but Agent Y called first. So I sign up with Agent Y? But I want Agent X? *What do I do?* Let me start by saying that this is a great problem to have. Then let me say that no, you do not have to sign up with the first agent that calls you and makes an offer. What you do have to do is behave in a way that is professional, respectful, and polite. When an agent calls and makes an offer of representation, it is well within your right to have a chat with that person, to "get to know them"—get a sense of what they're like, how they work, what their view of your project is, how they feel about the current status of your work, i.e., how much revision it needs, how many writers they represent, how long they've been in the business and so on. It's *okay* to ask. I encourage writers to ask me these questions; they should want to know who they are about to entrust their work to. And as for Agents X and Z, it's fine to let Agent Y know that you did a multiple submission, and you'll need to let the other players know that you have an offer of representation. This is totally reasonable. An open and honest dialogue is to be encouraged. How do you finally make your decision if you are lucky enough to be in a position to choose? It might be a gut feeling, or one agent's particular take on the material, or it might be because one agent happens to represent your favorite author, or maybe they represent a friend of yours and they come so highly recommended. The author/agent relationship is an incredibly personal one, and how you go about making that decision is totally up to you.

Do Literary Agents Lend Money and Bail Writers Out of Jail?

You have a literary agent! Congrats! But is part of you wondering, what exactly do they do? I mean, you get the general concept, that an agent is there to help you polish your work and sell it to a publisher, but is that really all? I have found that when I take on a new author, there is actually a lot of confusion about what exactly it is that an agent does.

What an Agent Does Not Do

I'll start off by telling you what an agent does not do. These are general parameters, of course. As soon as I tell you "a literary agent will not bail you out of jail," I'm certain I will hear a story of an agent who bailed a client out of jail. So, an agent is not required to lend you money if you decide to spend your advance on a car you can't afford, tell you an idea you have is good when it's clearly not, or tell you your pages are working when they aren't. An agent does not need to find you a new job because you decided to quit yours in order to write full time. In other words, an agent is not your personal assistant, therapist, or banker. That being said, many clients do develop very close personal relationships with their agents. It is undeniably a unique relationship, and it's not unusual for a close bond to form. Many of my clients were at my wedding, and I've attended the weddings of several of my writers. You become close when you work with people on such a personal level—but recognize that it can take time for these kinds of relationships to develop. If you start expecting this sort of closeness with your agent within five minutes of signing up with them, you're going to come off as intense and needy. Like any business relationship, take time to get to know the other person, and let friendship bloom over time.

What You Can Expect Your Agent to Do

While I promise I'll get into the details of the submission process in the next chapter, I think it's important for writers to know what exactly an agent's responsibilities to an author include. An agent's duties extend far beyond the actual submission process, and it can be helpful to have an idea of what your agent is going to do for you right from the beginning. Following is a list of some of the major responsibilities that an agent has to a client:

- Pre-submission preparation. An agent helps you get your work from point A to point B by giving you some guidance about your idea, your writing, and how to present it to a publisher. That being said, don't think you can just submit any old draft to your agent and expect them to fix it. If a client sends me something that isn't up to par, it goes right back. I expect the work they send me to be nearly ready for submission.

- Creating an appropriate submission list. Agents help you figure out which editors and publishers are right for your project.
- Negotiating deals and contracts. Agents should have extensive experience negotiating book contracts and be very familiar with the terms of these contracts. A good agent will work hard to get you the best possible terms.
- Selling subsidiary rights. Agents work with co-agents to sell foreign rights, film rights, and other ancillary rights to publishers.

How Does Your Agent Get Paid?

It is standard for literary agents to take 15 percent of your earnings. That means your agent will take 15 percent of your book advance and any royalties you earn, as well as 15 percent of any subsidiary deals they negotiate on your behalf, such as a movie deal. Agents will receive your check directly from your publisher. I know this sounds scary, but it's normal—this is how it works. Your agent will then write you a check minus their commission and any expenses you might have accrued during the selling of your work. Expenses are definitely something you should discuss with your agent. They can include the cost of shipping books, manuscripts, or proposals, or photocopying fees. Luckily, publishers are quite happy to receive e-mail submissions these days, so there are less expenses, but, again, this is something you'll want to discuss with your agent. And what if your book doesn't sell? Well then your agent doesn't make any money! That's why it is absolutely in our interest to make sure your book sells!

An Agency Agreement Is a Good Thing

Most agents will ask you to sign an agency agreement, which is basically a contract between you and the agency you have selected for representation. I happen to be a big fan of the agency agreement, and I think you should be too. An agency agreement is not about covering the agent's butt (if you're signing with a reputable agent), but about explaining the ins and outs of how the agency works, i.e., what they charge for commission, what their termination policy is, what they charge for expenses, etc. It is important that you know all of this information before you sign with an agent, so why not have it all spelled out in an agreement? Be sure to discuss anything that isn't clear with your agent before signing the agreement. I am always more than happy to explain anything in my agreement at length with a potential client and you should take an agent's willingness to do so as a good sign.

Your Agent Is Your Advocate

Perhaps the most important thing an agent does for you is to be your advocate from the time you submit your manuscript to a publisher, to the time you get your first offer, and even to that book landing on the shelves at the local bookstore. Anytime you have a question, issue, or concern about anything pertaining to your book, it's your agent who will go to bat for you. Your agent is there to guide you through the entire process, and that means helping you navigate any bumps along the way (and believe me, there will be bumps). But the challenges will all be worth it the very first time you see that book of yours on the shelf!

CHAPTER FOURTEEN:

Your Book's Publication From Point A to Point B

ou did it. You worked diligently on your memoir, you found an agent, revised your project, and what feels like a million years later, it's ready to be submitted to publishers. So what exactly happens? Does your agent "get on the horn" and start calling every editor in town to tell them how great of a writer you are? Then a few hours later, will a contract appear and you're on your way to becoming a published writer? Not quite. While your agent will certainly sing your praises, the process doesn't usually work that way (and while a book occasionally does get snapped up right away, don't think for a second you're going to get your contract that quickly). How does it work? This chapter will walk you through the entire process from point A to point B.

THE SUBMISSION LIST

Your agent will need to make decisions about which imprints are most appropriate for your project. It's also possible that your agent may have been talking about your project at lunch dates over the past couple of months while you were revising your work. I always keep a list of projects I have in the works and which editors have expressed interest in them. When it's time to make a submission, I look to see which editors have said they'd like to see that particular work. I also like to make an "A list" and a "B list." My A list might have five publishers on it, or as many as ten—it really depends on the project. Talk to your agent about her plans. How widely does she plan to submit your work? Who is she sending it to? I'm always happy to share my submission plans with my clients. They've been waiting for this moment for a long time, so I'm happy to keep them clued in on this part of the process.

Waiting for a Response Is a Lot Like Waiting for a Crush to Call

There is nothing worse than waiting to hear back from a publisher about your work. It's absolutely terrible. One client has told me she has to do everything in her power not to sit around in her house and "chew on the furniture." It can take awhile to hear back; editors are busy people, and rather than sitting by the phone waiting for your agent to call, it's generally best to keep busy. This is why I always tell clients to start thinking about that next project, or better yet, start working on it! In addition to keeping your mind occupied, I think it creates good vibes, who knows, that phone could ring any time, and an editor could very well want to know what your next project is! Maybe the interested editor will want to sign you for a two-book deal. It can't hurt to be prepared. What doesn't help is sitting around staring at the phone. We've all sat around waiting for a boy or girl we like to call, and has that ever done anyone any good? Staring at the phone never actually makes it ring. Do yourself a favor and start writing book number two.

Dealing With Rejection: It's Going to Happen

You need to know that there is not a writer on the planet who hasn't dealt with rejection. It hurts, but it's going to happen and you need to be prepared for it. I usually warn my authors that it isn't unusual for the first few responses from editors to actually be rejections—and that's okay. It's part of the process and every published writer has been through it. Here are a few tips for getting through this difficult but inevitable part of the submission process:

1. Don't obsess or overanalyze your rejection letters. It isn't unusual for each and every letter to be completely different. In other words, what bothers editor A is in fact editor B's favorite part of the book. If you revise your book every time an editor makes a comment, you will end up revising your book many times throughout this process. My rule of thumb was always that unless nearly every editor had the same issue, forge on.

2. Remember, a handful of rejection letters is nothing to worry about. If your agent is becoming concerned, she'll let you know. A few rejection letters is no reason to halt a submission. Don't panic.

3. It only takes one "yes" to make you a published author. Really, that's all you need. And only one "yes" is all it takes to become a huge best-selling author!

QUICK TIP: *I know it's easy to say, "Don't take rejection personally," but you really do need to remember how subjective these things can be. While your agent will do her absolute best to find an editor who is an excellent match for your work, finding that perfect editor for you involves not just finding someone who loves your work, but timing, too. Yes, the editor might love memoirs about families living on farms and raising chickens, but wow, wouldn't you know that yesterday he just bought a novel about a guy who gives up his corporate job to raise chickens? That's just too many chickens for one editor's list. Stranger things have happened when selling a book. Trust me, timing is everything.*

SOMEONE LIKES ME!
REALLY REALLY LIKES ME!

Finally, the phone rings. It's your agent. Someone likes your book! What happens next? When an editor falls in love with your book, it's not always easy to predict what the next steps will be. Generally speaking, your agent will use this interest as an opportunity to check in with all of the other parties who are considering your book. Where are they in the process? Have they read the materials yet? Your agent will be able to use Editor X's interest as leverage to get everyone else to pull out your project and put it on top of their pile of submissions. But what you need to know is this. An editor doesn't necessarily get to buy a book just because they love it. Buying a book requires support from an entire team of people at a publishing house—the editorial staff, the marketing team, the sales force, as well as publicity. All of these departments need to be on board before an offer is made. So essentially, *everyone* needs to fall in love with your book. It's a little intimidating right? So how does this work? The editor who is considering your book will present your work at an editorial meeting. This is a weekly meeting publishers have to discuss new acquisitions. Everyone weighs in with opinions on your material, your marketability as an author, your platform, and ultimately your book's likelihood of succeeding. So yes, of course, falling in love with your book is a big part of the equation, but it's also about how many copies of your book they're going to be able to sell.

When Editor X and Editor Y Both Want Your Book: The Auction

There is nothing more wonderful than having more than one editor who wants to buy a client's book. Being able to auction rights to an author's book is great fun—and, obviously, very exciting for the author. Who wouldn't be thrilled to have so much interest in their book? An auction happens when more than one publisher wants to buy rights to a book. Your agent can basically handle this situation in a number of ways. There are "best bids" auctions, where each publisher involved submits the highest bid they are willing to pay, and there are bids that go in "rounds" where each publisher calls in with a bid. Rules are preset in such auctions, such as the lowest bidder in each round is dropped; the rules are set by the individual agent depending on the situation.

Auctions Aren't Just About the Money

While it's exciting to have multiple publishers interested in your work, keep in mind that when choosing a publisher, it's not just about money. You'll need to talk to your agent about which publisher has the best "vision" for your book. What does that mean? You'll want to know how a publisher wants to "position" your book. Do they see it as a lead title? A hardcover or paperback? When do they want to publish? How much publicity and marketing are they willing to do? You'll also want to know about how they feel about the material. Obviously, they love it if they want to make an offer, but do they see it going in any particular direction? How closely will your editor be working with you to take it there? How does your book fit in with the rest of the titles on their list? How many titles do they publish each season? Will you be one of five or one of twenty? Ultimately, you want to make sure that the publisher you choose, in addition to making you an attractive financial offer, is also going to publish your work in the best way possible.

The Offer: What Exactly Will That Include?

This is the moment you've dreamed about ever since you realized you wanted to be a writer. What will it feel like to have a publisher tell you they are actually going to pay you to publish your book? I can't tell you how many authors have told me that they don't care how much the advance is—they'd let a publisher have the rights for free. They just want to see their book on the shelves! Well, a few months down the road, once that contract comes with its endless pages of language about royalties and subsidiary rights, they start to feel differently. Once an author sees how difficult it can be to earn back even a modest advance, the game changes. So be sure to educate yourself as much as possible about the deal you are agreeing to. Talk to your agent about the specifics the publisher is offering. Remember, publishing books is a business and you are a *businessperson*. Here's a rundown of the basics to familiarize you with what your publisher will be offering you.

Advance

Your advance is an amount of money your publisher is offering you against future earnings. In other words, if your publisher offers you an advance of $30,000, that's an advance of $30,000 against royalties. You will not receive a royalty check until your book has earned $30,000 in royalties.

Royalties

The amount of money you receive for each book. You may receive royalties on the "cover price" of the book or you may receive royalties on "net proceeds."

Standard hardcover royalties are:
- 10 percent of the cover price on the first five thousand copies sold
- 12.5 percent of the cover price on the next five thousand copies sold
- and 15 percent of the cover price thereafter

Standard trade paperback royalties are:
- 7.5 percent of the cost of the cover price

Standard mass market royalties are:
- 8 percent of the cost of the cover price on the first 150,000 copies sold
- and 10 percent thereafter

Royalties on a net proceeds basis will vary depending on the publisher. There are also various royalties paid out for subsidiary rights. Make sure you ask your agent if everything is "standard."

A Word About Small Advances: The Glass Is Half Full!

I realize there are many advantages to large advances: paying off bills, putting your kids through college, buying a totally impractical car. I get it. But in this challenging market, a large advance is much harder to come by, especially for a first-time author. I just wanted to point out that small advances have their advantages. No, you won't be able to pay off your mortgage—unless you decide to risk it all and you win big in Vegas, and that just doesn't sound wise. However, a small advance has the obvious advantage of being much easier to earn out than a large advance. If your first book advance is ten thousand dollars, with some hard work you'll be able to earn out, and your publisher will be as pleased as punch. Better yet, you'll earn royalties, your publisher will be even happier, and you'll be paving the way for a larger second book deal. And isn't that the point? A career of writing books? Who wants to be a one-trick pony?

Territory

When a publisher makes an offer, they are also making an offer on a territory, meaning where they are allowed to publish the book. Generally, a publisher will make an offer for "North American rights," "World English," or "World Rights." If your publisher is buying North American rights, your agent will reserve the right to sell your work in foreign territories. This means your agent will use his team of co-agents to sell your work in foreign markets. When a deal is made, your agent will split a 20 percent commission with the co-agent, and nothing will go to your U.S. publisher. If your U.S. publisher wants to retain foreign rights and makes you an offer for "World Rights," that means they would like to use their in-house rights team to license your work in foreign territories. Don't panic, this doesn't mean you don't get any more money. Let's say your publisher sells your work in France. Your publisher will keep 25 percent of the sale and give you 75 percent of the sale, but will put your portion of it toward earning back your advance. So you don't get the money up front, which can be a bummer. However, sometimes if a publisher suspects they can earn an advance back through foreign sales, they will be more likely to make an author a larger offer.

And for World English? That means the U.S. publisher has the right to license the book in English-speaking territories around the world. Same deal, but different split. If your publisher sells your book in the United Kingdom, they will give you 80 percent of the proceeds, but again, that money is going into your royalty account and you won't get a check until that advance is earned back. Please note however, that while the splits I've mentioned above are "industry standard," some publishers are of course going to deviate from the standard. But what I've outlined should give you a good sense of how territories and royalty accounts work.

Contracts

The contract always takes longer to arrive than an agent would like. It also takes longer to negotiate than we would like. Why does this matter so much? Because you won't be paid a single cent until that contract is signed. Now you want that contract to come a little bit quicker don't you? Don't worry, your agent will be on top of your publisher and will do everything she can to get your contract negotiated (remember agents don't get paid until you do). Just remember, while your agent will want this process to go as quickly as possible, it's your agent's job to make sure that you are signing a good contract. The process can't be rushed to the point where your contract is going to suffer. You also need to know what a "pay out" is. This is also part of the negotiation process. When your publisher makes an offer, they will tell your agent how much of your advance will be paid on signing and how much will be paid on "delivery and acceptance" of the manuscript—in other words, once you've turned the book in, your editor has read the manuscript, made comments, and you've incorporated the changes. Sometimes there will also be a payment on publication of the book. In the event of an especially large advance, there is sometimes also a payment on paperback publication. So while you'll be receiving a payment on the signing of your contract, just keep in mind it's not going to be your entire advance!

THE REVISION PROCESS

Editorial Letters and Copyediting

Perhaps the most exciting part of the process (or the most fun) is working with your editor on revisions. Each editor will have a different way of working, and it's important that you discuss her process with her. She may want you to deliver chapters for early feedback or half of the manuscript or she may not want to see anything at all until your official due date because of an especially busy schedule. Generally, you'll turn in your manuscript and receive what is known as an "editorial letter." Your editorial letter will detail any developmental big picture edits your book might have, any smaller tweaks you might need to deal with, and may also include a line edit (although some editors prefer to do those at a later stage). Everyone works differently. Some editors write quite a few detailed notes in their actual letter, while marking some notes on the physical manuscript or in Track Changes on the Word document. Other editors keep their letters shorter and will give you more detailed notes on your manuscript. Whatever their method is, it's always thrilling to work with someone who is an expert and is invested in making your book the best work it can possibly be.

Do I Have to Agree With Everything?

No. You don't have to agree with every change your editor suggests. What I usually recommend is reading through all of the notes and edits and then putting the entire thing away! Let the suggestions sit and give your brain some time to digest everything your editor is saying to you. This is especially true if you're the kind of writer who might have a strong reaction to criticism. The worst thing you can possibly do is sit down at your computer and pound out an e-mail to your editor about how she "doesn't understand your work" or "you just can't be on board with any of the edits." Take a breath. Look at the edits again tomorrow and see how you feel. If you're still concerned about the direction the editor is taking your work, call your agent! That's what they are there for—to help you navigate these tricky waters and to stop you from making a big mistake.

I'd also like to point out that while you are, of course, the writer, and the book is your baby, you do need to remember that your publisher wants your book to succeed. They are on your side! While you don't have to agree with every suggestion your editor makes, it can be wise to choose your battles. Your editor loves your book and wants it to sell as much as you do. Remember this as you are reading over the letter that she carefully and thoughtfully crafted.

Copyediting is the next step. Once you've incorporated all of your editor's suggestions, she'll pass your work off to a copyeditor who will review your manuscript for formatting, style, and accuracy. As I write this paragraph, I am absolutely terrified of what my manuscript will look like when it comes back from the copyeditor. I try to be diligent, *as should you* about grammar and punctuation, and I try to be as consistent as possible, but the bottom line is I'm terrible with such things and need to depend on an eagle-eyed friend for help with proofreading. It's actually helpful to make yourself a style sheet listing how you're going to deal with certain items throughout your book. Are certain things always bold? Italics? Memoirists can take this one step further. Are you changing names for privacy purposes (more on that in the next chapter by the way)? Then you need to make sure that Veronica doesn't become Victoria halfway through the manuscript. But if you forget (and I totally would), it's your copyeditor who is going to notice.

Book Jackets, Flap Copy, and Catalog Copy: Meet Your Friends in Sales and Marketing

Seeing your book jacket for the first time is a thrill (unless you don't like it of course) and more on that soon. Reading catalog and flap copy—and knowing that actual readers will soon be holding your book in their hands and reading those words to learn what your book is about—is an amazing feeling. So who is in charge of all this stuff? The process varies from house to house, but sales and marketing—the people who are dealing with booksellers every day—play a very important roll in shaping how your book is taken to market. Your editor helps too, but sales and marketing are the ones who ultimately make the decision about how your book is positioned. How will readers respond to the title? What kind of impact will the jacket have? Is the copy getting the message across? Sales and marketing are the people *who know*.

So what happens if you open that e-mail with your book jacket design and your heart drops? The design just isn't what you had in mind and it doesn't fit in with the vision you had for your book at all? Are you out of luck? It totally depends on your publisher and the stipulation of your contract, but more often than not, your publisher will want you to be happy with your book jacket. That being said, your publisher also needs your book to have a cover that they feel has a saleable design. The number one rule with anything you're not pleased with—whether it's jacket copy, catalog copy, or your actual book jacket is this: Don't react. Put it aside and think before you respond. It's always a good idea to ask your agent for an opinion and help with crafting a response—or asking her if she'd prefer to respond on your behalf. Remember, e-mails can't be taken back! It's your book, it's important, but it's always key to be professional, calm, and clear when stating your position. And here's another cliché that's true: You do catch more flies with honey than with vinegar. Being nice and courteous with your response is going to go a long way toward getting what you want.

> **REALITY CHECK:** *One of the most frustrating phone calls or e-mails an agent can get is from a client whose calling to say, "I happened to drop by a Barnes & Noble while on vacation in Anchorage, Alaska, and they don't carry my book!" It's true, as hard as the sales force at your publisher will work, not every bookstore will stock your book. Unless you are Stephenie Meyer or Stieg Larsson, there are very few authors whose books are carried in every single store. But know that the harder you work to sell your book, and the more copies you manage to move, the more likely it is that more stores will carry your book.*

CHAPTER FIFTEEN:

Controversy: "Navigating the Difficult Waters of Memoir Writing

 ames Frey's *A Million Little Pieces* was released by Doubleday Books in 2003 to mixed reviews. In 2005, the book was selected by Oprah Winfrey for her book club, and the memoir instantly became a *New York Times* bestseller. But in early 2006, *A Million Little Pieces* garnered widespread attention for an entirely different reason. After a detailed investigation, *The Smoking Gun* published an article called "A Million Little Lies" which provided a detailed account of the inaccuracies in Frey's story. Not only were stories of his arrests and jail time wildly exaggerated, but that he had also fabricated a story about undergoing a root canal without Novocain and his involvement in a tragic train accident that occurred in the town he grew up in. The end result of all this? A second visit on the Oprah show that included, as David Carr of *The New York Times* described it, "Both Mr. Frey and Ms. Talese (the publisher of his book) were snapped in two like dry winter twigs," a painful interview with Larry King, and the author's publisher offering a refund to anyone who felt they had been defrauded. My local library, the main branch of the Brooklyn public library, actually reclassified the book and moved it to the fiction section.

While *A Million Little Pieces* is perhaps the most infamous example of a memoir that didn't turn out to be all it claimed,

Margaret B. Jones' 2008 memoir *Love and Consequences*, about her life growing up in South Central Los Angeles as a half-white, half-Native American foster child in a street gang was found to be completely fictional shortly after it was published. Margaret Seltzer (her real name) was actually white, grew up in the affluent Sherman Oaks section of Los Angeles with her family where she attended private school. Seltzer's story fell apart after she was profiled in the *House and Home* section of *The New York Times*. Her sister saw the profile, obviously knew her story wasn't true and contacted Riverhead Books to inform them. Riverhead immediately recalled all copies of *Love and Consequences*. The list of memoir writers who have come under scrutiny in recent years is quite long. Augusten Burroughs was involved in a lawsuit with the family he lived with in *Running With Scissors*, the validity of Ishmael Beah's memoir *A Long Way Gone: Memoirs of a Boy Solider* has been questioned, and *Misha: A Mémoire of the Holocaust Years* by Misha Defonseca was discovered to be a fake Holocaust memoir.

Obviously Frey and Seltzer are the most extreme examples, but how much room is there in a memoir for deviation from the truth? The real answer is that no, there isn't room to deviate from the truth—but that being said, you are writing a memoir, not an autobiography. The bottom line here is that while many memoir writers will refer to journals, letters, or other such items for inspiration, no one is doing hard-core fact checking. If your memoir contains a scene about your junior prom, I highly doubt you're going to track down the principal of your high school to confirm that it was in fact "Mrs. Smith" who busted you for smoking in the parking lot and that she was wearing blue shoes. That being said, the core of your story is obviously expected to be true. While certain aspects of Frey's story may have contained some truth, it is clear that the book should have been sold and marketed as a novel. But what happens when you're just not sure if your family had turkey or ham for Christmas dinner 1982? Is your sister going to remember that it was in fact ham and your entire story is going to come under scrutiny and you'll end up in a hostile interview with Larry King? Most likely not. It's unrealistic to think you can remember all of the details of your life so vividly, but this obviously becomes more of an issue when you're talking about events that make up the foundation of the story you're telling—or perhaps involve someone else who plays a role in your story. What to do?

If you have some particular concerns about your memoir, you should be sure to discuss them with your agent or publisher. They may have specific ideas about how they would like to handle your story. However, there are some general instances when it is a good idea to consider adding a disclaimer or author's note into your memoir:

- if you want to mask the identify of certain people who appear in your story
- if you are concerned that certain memories are not 100 percent accurate, such as memories from childhood
- if you are planning on merging characters together (This can be tricky business, so you should absolutely make sure you discuss this with your agent and editor.)

HOW TO HANDLE DIFFERENT MEMORIES AND GENERALLY STAY OUT OF TROUBLE

It isn't reasonable to expect that a writer would remember every detail of his life with complete clarity. I'm not even sure what I ate for breakfast this morning. And when turning your story into a narrative, it can be necessary to rely on your memory to the best of its ability. Please note that I'm not suggesting you fill in holes of your story with what you would have *liked to happen*. If you're writing about your experience in the Peace Corps and you can't remember what you did during those three boring weeks where it did nothing but rain, you can't go making up a story about fighting off a pack of lions. It may also be necessary to point out that your version of a story may differ from someone else's. How likely is it that four family members will recount the exact same version of a vacation? Your version will likely be quite different from your younger brother's. That's the point of memoir—it's *your story*. Different memoirists have handled this in different ways. Following are some examples:

TENDER AT THE BONE: GROWING UP AT THE TABLE BY RUTH REICHL

In *Tender at the Bone: Growing Up at the Table*, Ruth Reichl opens with an "Author's Note." She starts off by saying that "storytelling, in my family was highly prized" and then goes on to tell a story about how her father, lacking a babysitter and needing to catch a train, had dropped her off at the age of two at a school she was too young to actually attend, and simply told her to tell the teachers she was there to "go to school" when they showed up. Reichl explains how she grew up believing this story, and she knows her father absolutely did, but as an adult she knows it simply isn't possible. She says that her book is "absolutely in the family tradition." Everything "is true but may not be entirely factual." She explains that she has compressed events, made two people into one, and "occasionally embroidered." Reichl is being clear and upfront with her intentions. The book is listed as a memoir, and is indeed an account of the author's early life with food. However, she had to be careful about how she presents her information. The basis of this book is truth, but she's letting us know that, every now and then, something is going to occur that she just can't possibly verify.

A HEARTBREAKING WORK OF STAGGERING GENIUS: A MEMOIR BASED ON A TRUE STORY BY DAVE EGGERS

Dave Eggers' story of losing both of his parents to cancer within thirty-two days of each other and being left to raise his younger brother Toph when he was in his early twenties was one of the most talked about books of 2000. Eggers' work was creative, fresh—and yes, it was heartbreaking. But was it a memoir? Right on the cover it says "based on a true story," and in his highly unusual acknowledgements in the opening pages, he tells a story about how he runs into a friend and explains that he's working on a "memoir-y kind of thing." Yet it takes quite awhile for the reader to have any reason to think this book is anything other than your standard, everyday kind of memoir. The opening chapter deals with Dave and his sister taking care of his mother—and all seems relatively normal. However, Eggers has pointed out to his readers that parts of his book were in fact fictionalized or exaggerated. In certain places, it's incredibly clear where this is happening—in others it's less so. Because Eggers felt that this venture into exaggeration or full-fledged fiction was a device that *enhanced his own story*, it was important that he was clear and upfront about it. Calling the book "based on a true story" takes care of that issue nicely.

MEMOIRISTS SHARE THEIR FAVORITE MEMOIRS

JIM KNIPFEL: AUTHOR OF *SLACKJAW*

I've come to prefer "memoirs in disguise." That is, memoirs disguised as novels. They tend to be much more truthful. So let me give you three favorites—two in disguise, one straight.

1. Henry Miller, *Black Spring*. A memoir disguised as a collection of personal essays, this was the very first book that not only excited me, but showed me that maybe writing was something I could do. The opening essay, "The Fourteenth Ward," is a masterpiece of both language and memory.

2. Louis-Ferdinand Céline, *Complete Works*. Throughout his writing career, Céline created and developed a style like no other, writing memoirs disguised as novels (or vice-versa), simultaneously tracing what happened externally as well as internally. People say his books are impossible and insane, but you just need to learn to think like him, which I guess some people might find a pretty scary idea.

3. Ryan Knighton, *C'mon Papa*. In general, I'm no fan of daddy books, but Knighton's is something quite different. Yes, the hook is that he's a blind father dealing with the birth of his first child. Well and beyond that, though, he's one of the best, sharpest, and funniest storytellers around today, whatever the subject matter.

REALITY CHECK: *Publishers don't have fact checkers. I know this may sound shocking (as it was to Oprah Winfrey and everyone in her studio audience the day James Frey paid his second visit), but publishers simply do not have the money to have a fact-checking department. You are responsible for your own fact checking. In fact, when you sign your contract, there is a clause that basically states that what you are writing is in fact true, and you are not libeling anyone. I know I just got done explaining to you that you don't need to follow up on your junior year prom date—and you don't—but you need to do your homework and make sure you are being a responsible writer and that the spine or foundation of your story is true! Do know that while most publishers will have an in-house attorney do a "legal vetting" to make sure you aren't going to be sued by anyone for libel, it's not the same thing as fact checking as some recent incidents indicate.*

Is Your Story All Yours?

When eighteen-year-old Joyce Maynard wrote the essay in *The New York Times* "An 18-Year-Old Looks Back on Life," I think it's safe to say that she never suspected its publication would lead to her dropping out of Yale to move in with the reclusive author of *The Catcher in the Rye*, J.D. Salinger. Salinger was one of many who wrote to Maynard as a result of that piece. The two eventually met, moved in together, and had what could be described as a bizarre and tumultuous affair. The much older Salinger quickly tired of Maynard and he asked her to leave. Maynard went on to marry, have several children and create a career writing columns, personal essays, and novels, while as well all know, Salinger was rarely heard from. Despite her commercial success, the one thing that the name Joyce Maynard was forever associated with was J.D. Salinger and their nine-month affair. And while Maynard wrote about everything from getting breast implants to diaper genies (she had two kids in diapers and needed money), she chose to remain silent on the issue of Salinger—until she was forty-four. When Maynard published *At Home in the World* about her experience living with J.D. Salinger in 1998, many felt that because her story involved such a famous writer that she had no right to tell *her story*. Maynard describes her experience during the publication of her memoir in an afterword in the newly released edition of *At Home in the World*: "The attacks, not only on my memoir, but also on my character, were brutal, intensely personal and relentless. I was called an exploiter, a predator. I lost count of the times I was described as 'shameless.'" And while it may be safe to assume that many of you who are reading this book did not have affairs with famous authors, the bottom line is that we all ultimately share our stories with others. So what exactly makes a story ours? This is perhaps one of the most complicated questions a memoirist must ask herself. And while there isn't a simple or easy answer to this question, I do believe that we do have a right to tell our own stories.

Larissa MacFarquhar wrote a piece called "The Cult of Joyce Maynard" for *The New York Times Magazine* on the release of *At Home in the World*. MacFarquhar met Maynard at her son's tennis tournament, and they talked about the publication of her book. Maynard described how writing the book had been like "the exorcism of a past that has been festering for years." "When I first embarked on it, it felt like such a forbidden thing, like my grandfather eating pork." Maynard then goes onto say, "But now I've come to feel there's nothing so terrible about truth, and it's such a relief." Even though Maynard underwent intense scrutiny for her choice to write about her time living with Salinger, she was able to take ownership of the fact that she was finally telling her story. The time she spent living with Salinger involved her life just as much as it involved his—why must she remain silent?

She goes on to say in her afterword to *At Home in the World* that "The truth is not always a comfortable thing to look at squarely. I don't know what we can ever learn, or how we are fully to understand human experience, if we fail to examine it. There is catharsis, of course, in exhuming a buried part of our lives. But more important, at least to me, was exploding the myth that any human being owes another human being her silence, at the expense of her ability to know and be her own true self."

If there is anything that can be learned from the reading and writing of memoir, it's this. Life is complicated. It isn't neat—and it certainly doesn't always show humanity at its best. But memoir is also where we see the human spirit surviving, making grave mistakes and hopefully recovering and learning from them. If writers didn't have the courage to do what Joyce Maynard did, I don't imagine there would be a single decent memoir to read at all.

COMING OUT OF THE MEMOIR WRITING CLOSET: AN INTERVIEW WITH HOLLIS GILLESPIE

Hollis Gillespie is the author of *Trailer Trashed: My Dubious Efforts Toward Upward Mobility, Bleachy-Haired Honky Bitch: Tales from a Bad Neighborhood,* and *Confessions of a Recovering Slut: And Other Love Stories.* She has been profiled in *Marie Claire, BUST, Entertainment Weekly,* and *Writer's Digest,* which named Hollis a "Breakout Author of the Year." Hollis is also known for her sellout writing seminars in the Atlanta area, so I thought she'd be the perfect person to ask about some of the stickier situations a memoir writer has to deal with.

1. How do you break the news to family/friends that you are writing a memoir? This seems like a frightening proposition.

It depends, but one thing is for sure: Some you thought would support you will abandon you and some you thought would abandon you will support you. That is an absolute given. Just wait and see. It's always a surprise.

2. At what point in the process is it wise to do this?

I wouldn't break the news until just before it's published. In fact, I recommend to my students that they should write it as though no one will ever read it. Because, seriously, have you ever tried writing ANYTHING with the judgment of an imaginary audience weighing you down? It's almost not possible, or if it were, what comes out is a complete adulteration of your natural narrative. So you have to put thoughts of judgment at bay and write it as though you are the only one who will ever see it. You will have plenty of time to worry about what people will think once you have your book advance and a publisher behind you. At that point, I dare you to let your fears win.

3. How do you recommend dealing with a negative reaction?

The only way to deal with it is to let them have their say. You had yours, so it's only fair. Be strong, and take comfort in the fact—the absolute fact—that no two people ever recall the same event in the same way. Personally, I remember what my sister, who used to be a bailiff in the San Diego County Court System, said to me once. She talked a lot with the defense attorneys, and they told her that the most easily refuted testimony is eye-witness testimony, because no two people's memories ever completely coincided. (And my sister will probably read this and say, "I never said that!" Hahahaha!)

RECOMMENDED READING

UNIQUELY HANDLED MEMOIRS

A Heartbreaking Work of Staggering Genius by Dave Eggers

At Home in the World by Joyce Maynard

"To Be Perfectly Honest: Why Fiction Can Be More Truthful Than Memoir," Essay, *New Haven Review* by Jim Knipfel

Acknowledgments

If there's one thing I've learned while working in book publishing it's this. It's an absolute privilege to write a book. It takes the help of many wise people—publishing professionals as well as supportive friends and family. I'm extraordinarily fortunate to have had the help of many.

I'd like to thank Scott Francis at Writer's Digest for being an all-around fantastic editor. Patient, smart, funny, and full of good ideas. It was a great first experience for me and I'm grateful to him for making me a better writer. I'm also thankful to Kelly Messerly and Claudean Wheeler from the Writer's Digest family as well as Jane Friedman and Kelly Nickell. Thank you to Suzan Colon, Kelly Corrigan, Melissa Houtte, Jim Knipfel, Kirk Read, and Amy Wilson for sharing their favorite memoirs with me. The time and effort you gave made this book better.

I wouldn't know any of the stuff I've written about in this book were it not for my teachers and clients I've learned so much from over the years. Thanks to Stuart Krichevsky, Michael Carlisle, and Sarah Lazin. I'd also like to give a special shout-out to Alexandra Robbins who is not only an incredible writer and overall swell individual—but who happens to write the best acknowledgments in the history of book publishing. I'm happy to have a chance to throw one her way.

Who could write a book without family and friends? I would never have written a book without the support of my wonderful husband Peter, who knew I would write one from day one. June, see? Mom really does work! You are my Ramona. Thanks to Stephen Serwin for being THE best friend a girl could have since the age of four. How did I get so lucky? To David Halpern for always listening and providing the best advice and funniest conversations just when I need them most. And warmest of thanks to Dena Koklanaris, Billy Kingsland, and Jenna Johnson. The Vitale Clan—Ann, Meg, Sydelle and Nick, all of the Balzers, and especially my grandmother, Joan Balzer for encouraging my love of books. My parents Jan and Glen Loderhouse, John Balzer and Jacki King. My sister Stacy Balzer, Jake, Maya & Ashlee. And Brittani & Matthew Clark, and Jack. And Joan & Gary Joans with their help in spreading the word.

I'd also like to thank Carrie Harvey and Tonya Vernooy of adhocMOM without whom I never would have believed I could write a single word. You inspire me every day with your creativity and intelligence—and without your friendship, where would I be? And in that vein, the best women I know, Jill Penman, Erin Bogaty, Maya Baran (and for those lunches!), Joanna McFadden, and Jess Parsons. I wouldn't have survived my first year of motherhood without your love and support. You all make me a better person.

About the Author

 **PAULA BALZER** is a literary agent who has worked with Oscar-award winning writer of the screenplay *Juno*, Diablo Cody, *American Idol*'s Randy Jackson, *New York Times* best-selling author Alexandra Robbins, and author of the cult classic *Gospel of the Flying Spaghetti Monster*, Bobby Henderson. She is also a co-founder of the popular blog www.adhocmom.com. Paula has a particular fondness for memoirs and will read them on absolutely any topic. She lives in Brooklyn with her husband and daughter.

Index